Soul
TENDING

Soul

TENDING

A JOURNEY INTO
THE HEART
OF SABBATH

ANITA AMSTUTZ

Walking Together, Finding the Way®

SKYLIGHT PATHS®
PUBLISHING
Nashville, Tennessee

SkyLight Paths Publishing
an imprint of Turner Publishing Company
Nashville, Tennessee

www.skylightpaths.com
www.turnerpublishing.com

Soul Tending: A Journey into the Heart of Sabbath

For information regarding permission to reprint material from this book, please write or fax your request to Turner Publishing, Permissions Department, at 4507 Charlotte Avenue, Nashville, Tennessee, 37209 (615) 255-2665, fax (615) 255-5081, or email your request to submissions@turnerpublishing.com.

Library of Congress Cataloging-in-Publication Data available upon request.

18 19 20 21   10 9 8 7 6 5 4 3 2 1

Manufactured in the United States of America
Cover Design: Maddie Cothren
Interior Design: Tim Holtz

To my parents. You have lived faithfully,
handing me a firm foundation upon which to build.

CONTENTS

INTRODUCTION

We live in hungry times. A winter of sorts in our political and civic spheres. There is economic uncertainty, fear, violence, division, and social chaos. What is needed for times such as these is a heart full of courage and wisdom, grounded in compassion and resilience. For this, I turn to one of the practices that for so many centuries nourished people of faith through incredibly difficult life circumstances and service. Traditionally it was a communal gathering time—a coming together of rest, ritual, and prayer. It is Sabbath keeping.

I have come to know that without a dedicated time away, a ceasing of our labors and unplugging as Sabbath asks us to do alone or in community, we will come empty-handed and overwhelmed to face a world that is increasingly morally bankrupt, its illnesses legion. We stand on the turbulent precipice of global problems that imperil human survival on this planet—climate change, violence, rising tides of xenophobia, racism, poverty, misogyny, fear, and anxiety.

Humankind is desperate for answers and a new way of living in this time of cynicism, destruction, and greed. We hunger to be reawakened in all our senses to a deeper meaning and collective purpose. Our busyness belies the emptiness, ache, and lack of true connection we feel. We continue to wonder at a culture spinning out of control. Norman Wirzba, writer and professor at Duke School of Theology, talks about the fact that we are a restless, mobile society living "through" place rather than "in" place. Even more than rest, Sabbath keeping is about facing the deep roots of our restlessness. It is about facing "how it is"—our relentless lives that consume us, conspiring to keep us from the very intimacy we desire and from health and wholeness, shalom. We will not move into a new way of being from the same mindset, we must find time to envision new answers.

But even greater than the problems of living together as societies and our cultural issues is an economic system that rewards the wealth of a few at the expense of the multitudes. For the masses who must work long hours, double shifts with poor compensation and little to no retirement or time-off benefits, work has become dreary. For those lucky to have meaningful work, there will still be the tedium at times with the rat race, poor working environments, terrible colleagues, demanding bosses, or feeling overwhelmed. We have become trapped in an idea of work handed to us by the culture around us. I wonder if it's time to examine this.

Tending the Sabbath soul can reignite love and help a heart become flesh again for our daily work at hand—including justice making and healing our world. Practicing Sabbath keeping may actually call us to work outside the box. Perhaps more than Sabbath, this book is a commentary on work and what we've been taught to believe about it; how we participate in an economic system destroying so much of what we love and value—even as we enjoy the comforts and conveniences as a fortunate few. Reflecting on work in these times feels of critical importance. Becoming conscious of the purpose of our work in the world, its proper place and perhaps even reimagining work, may be the challenge of our times.

Soul Tending is my story about work and ceasing work. It is about the cycles of burnout followed by regular Sabbath keeping. Of world weariness and rejuvenation. Over a decade of pastoring, I found myself grappling with these things and seeking equanimity in my life—over and over. My own experience showed me that

Sabbath keeping could create a certain clarity, calling me to more robust and wholehearted living. It was about tending my own soul, even as I tried to do that for everyone else. As an ordained pastor, I finally came to keep Sabbath on Mondays and then during extended sabbaticals. The adventure of years trying to attend to this day of rest, with many failures and some successes, began to bear fruit somewhere along the way. Rabbi Michael Lerner says that you can't really know the fruits of this practice until you keep Sabbath weekly for at least a couple of years. I can attest to that. Like any spiritual practice, it grounded me, frustrated me, and finally grew me up.

Time spent at monasteries gave me the vision of a life that must be grounded in *ora et labora*, prayer and work. Prayerful work. The practice of Sabbath eventually brought me to a surprising conclusion in my life. My story and its ending in the book were only a new beginning for me, a birth of another kind in terms of my work in the world. It has reminded me that for the times we live in, we who are conscious and alive are called to examine our lives, to welcome ongoing transformation and yes, even re-invention.

Today my body and soul know when I am skipping my Sabbath. I am drawn back to it, like a moth to a flame. Indeed, at times it can sear my heart with its clarion call to give up all the ways I distract, manipulate, control, and allow myself to be overwhelmed in this society. Once Sabbath integrated into my life, my soul became more spacious and expansive—wider in its ability to hold beauty, sorrow, joy, and compassion at once.

Sabbath can help us retrieve joy from the dungeons of overwork, stress, and soul weariness. If individuals, families, parishes, congregations, synagogues, and communities practiced it collectively on a regular basis, children could be entrained in its wisdom and delight from a young age. Perhaps it would stick, instilling in them a spiritual practice that is actually not about denying oneself but rather about retrieving something life-giving. An "I get to," rather than a "should." It could change their understanding of what is their work to do in the world and how to go about their lives.

I didn't intend to write a book. You might say it wrote me. One Sabbath day, it took hold and poured out of me for the next few months. I can't say that I am offering anything particularly new, but I do think this book is timely. My story is only one piece of our shared human experience. Like a patchwork quilt, we all have a particular story to be told of our life and how we've lived it. Yet, as workers, whatever our vocation or lot in life, we all seem to be yoked in the same struggle. When time becomes scarce and the flames of joy, play, creativity, simplicity, hospitality (some of the themes in this book) die back, it is easy to lose a sense of meaning or purpose. Life becomes more burdensome and busy, lived in quiet desperation rather than joyousness and balance. In the midst of work, unexpected life circumstances still happen—leaving us hanging on by a thread. Sabbath can restore us to face the challenges of all of it. When we have more spaciousness in our lives, we have greater inner resources for facing what is at hand. We are present to the world around us in a new way. We can be sustained in our ordinary, workaday world where we spend most of the hours of our lives.

I write this simple book especially for people who humbly serve the common good each and every day of the week that you go out into the world. You will never be the top 1 percent of our society, thank goodness. Yet you are the glue that keeps our society from total meltdown. Even so, the struggles and challenges arrayed against ordinary mortals are monumental. We can no longer go out into the world expecting that our life will be untouched by the massive problems of the age. And as people of God, we should not be untouched. We are called to turn toward, not away from, the most vulnerable under siege—including all the living communities of the earth. We will sorely need a Sabbath mind and way of being in the chaos and social transformation that our culture is facing.

Since Sabbath is not just a solitary journey, but also about communities sharing time and space to mine their own hopes and dreams, this Sabbath keeping memoir includes a study guide at the end of each chapter. It can be used as a small-group conversation starter for professionals working in the trenches—a seminary, college, or Sunday school class primer on the intersection of Sabbath, work, and our lives. It can be a personal study book. Sabbath space creates time for reflection and renewal, conjuring up dormant dreams and the sowing of new seeds.

So, intrepid Sabbath keepers in this twenty-first century, I bring you treasures for ceasing work to tend your Sabbath soul from three monotheistic traditions: Islam, Judaism, and Christianity. Though I am well aware of the beautiful gems from many other spiritual traditions, these three are the taproot of my spiritual ancestry—arising from the story of Abraham, Sarah, and Hagar and their offspring. I offer this to you and your communities as a primer, a handbook of practice and reflection to deepen your own fortitude and compassion for our times.

See what might change for you as you make spacious time for a lived weekly Sabbath—and I'm not just talking about an hour of worship once a week at your local church, synagogue, mosque, or faith community. I'm talking about twenty-four hours. I can't stress this enough. It is in the regular practice of tending the Sabbath that the soul deepens into a Sabbath mind—a mind resting in divine peace and joy. People of great heart and faith are needed for these times, and tending the Sabbath soul is a powerful way to grow these spiritual muscles—solo and with others. So gather a group and practice together. Or begin the journey alone. But do take it up.

Unplug. Yes, you heard that right. Unplug from your techno toys for twenty-four hours. Every week. Go into the silence with the Divine Lover. Be with your own soul. Hang out with family and friends. Turn off the TV and be real with one another for a whole day. Play games. Take a long time making a meal together. Enjoy. Practice the art of conversation. Dance together. Spend time in the solace of the natural world. Not all of us can be monastics, but Sabbath keeping is where you can find the beating heart of the monastery.

Go into this timeless house of Sabbath, described by Rabbi Abraham Joshua Heschel as "a palace in time" and tend your soul. You will savor life more deeply. I guarantee it.

1

SIMPLICITY
Stripping Down Our Lives

An efficiently busy life that keeps us occupied
without being harried and keeps our attention
entirely on interesting outer things is probably
more potentially destructive of spiritual growth
than debauchery or alcohol or hard drugs. . . .
On the other hand, a quiet, efficient, and busy
life spent continuously in good works can shield
us effectively from any plunge into the depth
where the Divine can find us.
—MORTON T. KELSEY, *The Other Side of Silence*

HUMILITY

It had been a long dry season in ministry, with fractious, sorrow-ful, and difficult issues. I was a constant whirlwind of activity. Committee meetings at night. Individual meetings by day. Endless teaching, preaching, and administrative cycles. My bones some days felt as though they were turning to dust. My own personal crises had collected around the edges, converging with the challenges of pastoring. It was the perfect storm. Despite ten years of ministry under my belt, all my foregone conclusions about my pastoral identity and vocation were suddenly called

---

into question. I no longer had any answers for what was happening, for who I was becoming, and what or whom had chosen me. I was having a full-blown midlife crisis. It was the unbidden, classic dark night of the soul, not only for me but also for a whole community.

As the summer drew to a close, I knew I needed a break for health itself. It seemed like a courageous time to enter my inner landscape more fully, since it had languished for a long time. I needed to know more of my God-given vocation than just the set of ministerial credentials and identity markers I had been handed. My congregation was willing to let me go on an extended Sabbath, a time of sacred simplicity, during which I sought refuge in Christ in the Desert Benedictine Monastery, an outcropping of adobe buildings nestled in the orange, pinyon-dotted painted canyons of New Mexico.

As the AA community already knows, it takes at least ninety days of being clean and sober to change one's habits. And I had ninety days in my pocket for my sabbatical, the first ten of which would be spent with these monks. During this time I would begin to face my obsessive-compulsive need to "take care of" and "fix" everything in sight. I would begin to face my own hungers and wants—those things that compelled my need to acquire, exploit, dominate, and lead. It would be an exercise in humility as I stared down my own self-destructive habits—my own blind and unreflective nature—that, if left unchecked, might plunge me off the edge of my soul's sanity.

Benedictine oblate Christine Valters Paintner says humility is as foundational as the ground we walk on, as basic as the earth—or *humus*—we're made from:

> Humility is the fundamental recognition that we each draw our life and breath from the same source—the God who made us and calls us beloved. Humility prevents us from seeing ourselves as more deserving or graced than

another person. It also compels us to recognize that we are no less deserving or graced than another. Humility draws us into mutual relation, through which we allow no abuse, no demeaning, no diminishment of others or of ourselves. Through humility we can let go of the quest for perfection.[1]

Yes, this Sabbath would be humbling, a time to understand how these compulsions lived in me and to begin to inch toward shalom, wholeness. This was my chance to learn and put into place healthy habits that could sustain spiritual leadership. A time to cease my good works and become attuned to the deeper truth of my existence. As I walked away from my duties that summer, I was assailed by old ghosts that I had once carefully locked away underneath my daily life. It was not pretty. But I had time. Submitting to simplicity is always about humbling ourselves. A humility that comes from putting aside our agendas.

SURRENDER AND THE COST OF CHANGE

Our souls love simplicity. If you want to welcome your soul home, strip your life down to the bare bones. Watch your soul leap up and begin to play with all that spaciousness. Learn the wisdom of your soul that has been locked up for too long. In the special simplicity of Sabbath time, you quickly learn what to keep and what to release in your life, what makes you sick and what gives you cause to rejoice. It calls you to live an examined life. The soul is nourished by such open-ended time. That is something in short supply today.

Sabbath helps you simplify your life, and in today's culture such simplicity implies submission. It means giving up something for another thing. Submitting to a new reality. There is a beautiful German word that Anabaptists, forerunners of Mennonites, claimed for their sixteenth century Reformation movement: *Gelassenheit*. Surrender. A yieldedness to God.

We are not a culture that has been taught to submit or surrender. The new religion of our Western culture is our economy, and the best way to participate is with our paycheck. Our children are catechized in the school of the almighty dollar. In order to keep the machine of our economic system strong, we must consume constantly. We buoy ourselves up with material goods. We aim to acquire more, more, more. So we work harder. We have become hamsters running endlessly on our wheels of ambition.

Yet Sabbath calls us to submit our will, for the higher good of all, to a Higher Power. It asks us to slow down and pay attention not to the external prompts of consumerism but to the inner guidance of our souls. It challenges us to move beyond our comfort zones, to set aside our ego needs—those gnawing hungers for stuff, attention, praise, and being good enough. In a time of clamoring choices—more than we know what to do with—Sabbath says, "Stop." Ultimately it asks us to change our life.

In *Sabbath Resistance*, Episcopal priest and spiritual writer Barbara Brown Taylor states:

> Anyone engaging the practice of Shabbat can expect a rough ride for a couple of years at least. This is because Sabbath involves pleasure, rest, freedom and slowness, none of which comes naturally to us in North America . . . so sold on speed, invested in productivity, so convinced that multi-tasking is the way of life.[2]

Stopping can feel like a death, Taylor says, "as time billows out in front of you, you can have a little panic attack at how much of it you are wasting since time is not only money but also the clock ticking on your life."[3] Sabbath keeping is a moderating of the culture in order to find balance in one's life again.

The word *Islam* refers to both the religion of Muslims and the universal theme of self-surrender. For Muslims, Friday is designated as a day of rest for community, family, and prayer time. Sufi teacher and author Jamal Rahman speaks to this difficulty of surrender, how we often call out to God in our hour of need, only to return to our old habits and the trancelike unconsciousness of our life once the crisis has passed.

> We humans don't lightly alter our lifestyles, aspirations, and priorities. . . . We hide behind what Rumi calls the veils of health and wealth. When all is going well in our life, we pay little attention to spiritual matters. When the veils are ripped by, say, a cancer diagnosis, or a business failure, we may seek divine assistance, but when the crisis is over we quickly return to square one.[4]

God has extended to us an ongoing offer of priceless gems, but we must surrender our time and our energy in order to experience these consolations more than just in times of crisis.

PEELING BACK THE LAYERS OF BUSYNESS

During my extended Sabbath at the monastery, I learned why I didn't leave my life for such utter silence very often. I risked facing the suffering in my own inner landscape. I risked reckoning with the violence of the world around me that I kept at an arm's length daily. With my days stripped to be simply about waking up and getting out of bed, my emotional life began to flow like the incoming tide. The waves crashed against my carefully built levee of control: my denial.

Inside the thick adobe walls of my little monk's cell, where I lived for the next ten days, I was suddenly grief-stricken, washed away from the safe shoreline of my own construction. I had come because I wanted some answers. *How do I move into this second half of my life?* Middle age felt like a mile marker. I desired a more contemplative life and yet I had spent the last years as a spiritual leader of a growing faith community. I had honed my skills and served the community through sermons, administration (badly, at times), group process, individual counsel, conflict transformation work. But I had begun to feel as though my messages were falling flat and the fire of my passions was just snuffed-out embers.

At the monastery in the high desert, in that container of simplicity, I was finally able to wrestle with the particular angel that came to accompany me at that time. The Rule of Benedict, the guidebook for Western Christian monastic living written by Benedict of Nursia (c. 480–550 CE), speaks to moderation: "We are committed to practicing simplicity and frugality, to be content with living simply and finding balance in work, prayer, and leisure." For Benedictine monks and nuns, this is accomplished by a lifestyle that fosters peace and a simpler rhythm. I was invited to participate in the Daily Office, a rigorous schedule of collective prayer, often sung, seven times daily—Vigils at 4 a.m., Lauds at 5:45 a.m., followed by Eucharistic mass, Terce at 8:45 a.m., Sext at 1 p.m., None at 3:30 p.m., Vespers at 5:50 p.m., and Compline at 7:30 p.m. During this carefully balanced life of work, mealtimes, and regular prayer, I peeled away the onion skin of my world, and I was finally able to hear above the din of the city, above the din of my own obsessive-compulsive emotions. It was here that my soul found solace and courage—a way forward.

THE TRADITION OF SABBATH SIMPLICITY

Extended or not, this is what Sabbath does for us—the simplicity of retreat and routine bares our souls and bears us up amid the suffering of our existence. As early twentieth-century Christian mystic Evelyn Underhill describes:

I believe the retreat as a part of our normal spiritual routine will yield on the whole its fullest results when we regard it more often and more generally, in Abbot Delatte's beautiful phrase, as an opportunity of "steeping our souls in the beauty of the mysterious."[5]

Submitting weekly to the simplicity of the Sabbath is a spiritual practice of Jewish people, Christians, and Muslims, as I mentioned previously. The Sabbath, or *Shabbat* in Hebrew, is one of the most important days instituted by God in the Hebrew Bible. Literally meaning "to cease, to end, to rest," the Sabbath follows six task-oriented, building, and creating days with twenty-four hours of rest and spiritual enrichment on the seventh. The Ten Commandments call not only for remembering (Exodus 20:8) but also for observing Sabbath (Deuteronomy 5:12). For traditional Jewish people, the Sabbath is honored beginning at sundown on Friday and lasts until the first three stars show in the sky on Saturday evening. It is a highly prescribed day of rest, though some of the rules have relaxed over the centuries. Traditionally food is prepared ahead of time so no work would be required of anyone. Even the flip of a button or a switch could be seen as work.

The Sabbath imperative is to *not* accomplish or initiate anything, refuting the belief that you have to "do something" to be worthy. Instead, the original vision of Sabbath calls us to cease doing something, acquiring things, making stuff, expecting returns. Instead, we are called to just be and receive the Creator's good gifts. Forget stifling restrictions. Instead, time is savored as a precious gift from God. Time for your body to stretch and your soul to relax.

In the Christian New Testament, Jesus taught on multiple occasions about Sabbath keeping. He made it clear that Sabbath was made for humankind, not the other way around. Thus, Sabbath rules and regulations should never trump doing a kind deed or working on behalf of the Kingdom of God. For Christians, then, the meaning of Sabbath is as a time to offer ourselves up as a living sacrifice to God. It is a time to become more Christ-like—a vessel of love and healing for the world.

This way of keeping time on a simpler scale becomes a transformation of priorities and the affections of our heart. As author John D. Roth explains, "At its heart, Christian faith points toward a transformed understanding of reality itself. In Christian language, repentance (Greek *metanoia*) or conversion implies a fundamental 'turning around' . . . a fundamental change in our worldview."[6]

Christians traditionally observe Sabbath on Sunday. As a Christian minister, I learned that this day becomes a joyful opportunity to regularly wed ourselves to the Lord of the Sabbath. Sunday, as the first day of the week, symbolizes the day when the women disciples as eyewitnesses reported Jesus's resurrection from the grave. Sabbath is about an ongoing resurrection from the decay and death of our life and culture, a turning around and walking in the way of Jesus, the one who makes all things new. Sunday Sabbath, then, resets our souls.

Remembering the Gospel stories of Jesus through the elements of liturgy—word, song, Eucharist, baptism, prayer— becomes a clarion call for the gathered community to collectively return to the world to do the work of compassionate service, healing, peace, justice, and reconciliation. But if it becomes only a rote activity with no deeper change of heart, then, as the prophet Isaiah wrote, Sabbath is only a ritual, festival, or ceremonial law that God despises (see Isaiah 1:13).

Transformation is also at the heart of a true celebration of Jewish Shabbat. By submitting to a simpler rhythm for the day, letting go of the need to be in charge, the community slows down and unplugs from a culture that dominates and colonizes our collective headspace, giving us the illusion that we are in control. Giving up a day for Shabbat reorients our very lifestyle and heart.

In *Mudhouse Sabbath,* historian and writer Lauren Winner cuts to the heart of Sabbath meaning by recounting a story of the Konigsbergs, an Orthodox Hasidic family in Crown Heights, New York, who is visited by a secular Jew for Shabbat. Over dinner, their guest, Liz Harris, who is not just a little perplexed and annoyed by all the restrictions and rules, asks the Konigsbergs why God cares whether or not she microwaves a frozen dinner on Friday night.

"What happens when we stop working and controlling nature?" Moishe Konigsberg responds. "When we don't operate machines, or pick flowers, or pluck fish from the sea? . . . When we cease interfering in the world, we are acknowledging that it is God's world."[7]

Sabbath, then, reminds us whose world it is and with whom we co-create.

RETURN, RENEW, REPEAT

One day with Father John in the hops fields at the Benedictine monastery, I finally faced how un-simple my life had become, how far from the Holy Spirit I felt. I lived a very cluttered reality. The shallowness of my inner life lurked in the shadows constantly. Father John asked me if I prayed. Defensively I told him I *had* learned contemplative prayer and practiced it regularly at one time. Father John simply quoted from the book of Isaiah, "Return and renew again . . . "

Return. That is the point of Sabbath keeping. Father John then kneeled and bent over the dirt, using a metaphor appropriate for the farmer he is. He asked me to imagine filling a fifty-five-gallon drum with water from a hose. Then to imagine that I turn off the water but the drum keeps filling up. Now he sat on his haunches and showed me that he had opened an imaginary nozzle at the bottom of the drum. Water was pouring in from below, continuing to fill it up with water. "That is what prayer becomes, an external spring from below, filling you up!"

He quoted one of the early church fathers, Bernard of Clairvaux:

> If then you are wise, you will show yourself rather as a reservoir than as a canal. For a canal spreads abroad water as it receives it, but a reservoir waits until it is filled before overflowing, and thus communicates, without loss to itself, its superabundant water. . . . In the Church at the present day, we have many canals, few reservoirs.[8]

In my busy, hectic, frenzied life, I had become the canal keeper, trying to manage and send God's love to the right places. But that wasn't my job, evidently. I needed to allow myself to be filled up with God's love, through time set aside. The spillover would accomplish God's work in the world where it was most needed. Sabbath time allows me to become a reservoir, not a canal, overflowing with God's love. I can trust that as I cease work temporarily, it isn't the end of the world. The complexities of work and the people I serve await my return. They will be even better nourished if I return with a renewed vision and energy.

As I honor the Sabbath on Mondays, on my best-kept days I stop doing laundry. I leave the vacuum in the closet. I turn off all my electronic devices. I go down by the river for a three-hour walk. Sabbath becomes an opportunity for direct encounter, a lived experience of being in the presence of something greater than my small self. Prayer changes when I get out of my workaday space. If I am willing to submit to an unscheduled day, lay down my agenda, and show up, the day then becomes like an airy cathedral of timelessness. Some Mondays I muster up a whole day. Sometimes it is only a morning or an afternoon. I take comfort in the words of the anonymous author of the fourteenth-century English classic *The Cloud of Unknowing,* who wrote, "You only need a tiny scrap of time to move toward God."[9]

The sliced-and-diced days that become a string of endless, absolutely necessary activities suddenly fall away. My existence becomes rewoven together in a seamless, spacious whole. I take a deep breath and realize I don't have to be anywhere. I don't have to do anything. I only need to be present to my soul. I find myself moving and breathing in the greater soul of I AM. I have achieved Sabbath mind.

WHAT IS SABBATH MIND?

Sabbath mind is a fruit of regular Sabbath keeping. Whether you keep Sabbath as part of a religious community or on your own, the goal is to empty your mind out so that the Sacred can become apparent. The Sacred is often hidden under the vast quantity of information that comes as a blizzard each day. The Holy is buried under mounds of trivia and the details of our daily lives. Rabbi Abraham Joshua Heschel beautifully describes Sabbath mind as paired with sacred moments. We must loosen our grip on the daily diet of frantic overwhelm that we have come to think of as normal in our society. We must simplify our mind and life. Heschel writes:

> The higher goal of spiritual living is not to amass a wealth of information, but to face sacred moments. . . . Spiritual life begins to decay when we fail to sense the grandeur of what is eternal in time.[10]

Sacred moments. We all long for those glimpses beyond the curtain of time. Places and spaces in our daily lives when the veil becomes so thin that we are suddenly transported into the presence of the Sacred. Bathed in meaning. Washed clean by Love.

Anthropologists call this "in between" time, "liminal" space. Rigid psychological barriers or old ways of being or seeing can dissolve as we experience a revelation of the Divine. Rituals in any culture that mark birth, marriage, death, transition, healing, and worship, to name a few, can become times of unexpected transformation. An archetypal example of this is Moses and the burning bush. In Exodus 3:1–23 of the Hebrew Bible, Moses is tending his father-in-law's sheep in the desert. He has run away from an act of violence he committed, and he has been hiding out for years. Moses encounters a bush on fire and notices that the bush is not being consumed by the flames. So Moses comes closer. In that transcendent moment, he hears a voice calling from within the bush, telling him to take off his shoes, telling him he is on holy ground. It is this experience that shatters Moses open to the possibility that he can and will lead his people, the enslaved Israelites, out of Egypt into freedom. His own mind is emptied out enough that he can hear the still small voice of YHWH. He is experiencing a sacred moment, the beating heart of Sabbath mind.

It is rare that we can control or engineer such experiences. They come to us, often unbidden, in the midst of our greatest suffering, or when we fall in love—with a person, an animal, the beauty of creation, an idea. But we *can* manage how we use our time. How we spend our time is likely the single most important and powerful choice we have in this life. As the poet Mary Oliver states, to live simply is to choose what you will do with your one precious life. By choosing only a few from a multitude of things, you will burrow into what matters.

Sabbath mind cleaves to simplicity. It hungers for it and seeks a simpler life as a pearl of great price. Making space for a weekly Sabbath is one way to lead yourself home to your soul's deepest longing and desires. To transformation. To that place of a potential encounter with the Divine. Whether your soul is sickened, hopeful, tired, joyful, excited, lonely, grieving, or—as mine was at my midlife crossroads—searching, when you spend time with your soul, it will open up new, uncharted pathways. Your soul's landscape is rich with meaning. If you're like most of us, you rarely take the time to plumb these depths. But if you take the time for Sabbath regularly, I promise you that one day set aside will begin to recharge your life as you leave it empty. It will renew your body. It will deepen your relationships, including that with the Sacred Mystery. Sabbath practice and rhythm, spent with the intention of simplifying your life will, over time, bear the profound fruits of liminal moments and the graces of a life lived with purpose and meaning.

It will also bedevil you and open up doors you'd rather keep locked. For Sabbath keeping calls you to surrender and to the deepest humility. Peeling back the layers of busyness to even *see* those doors you'd rather not open takes great courage. But let's face it, the skeletons that we keep stored away will come calling with or without Sabbath keeping. At least with Sabbath keeping you will begin to build the fortitude of Sabbath mind. It will give you a buffer, an anchor. You will be ready, even when you are visited by a "crowd of sorrows that violently sweeps your house."[11]

Nineteenth-century German philosopher Friedrich Nietzsche writes:

> The essential thing "in heaven and earth" is . . . that there should be a long *obedience* in the same direction; thereby . . . has always resulted in the long run, something which has made life worth living; for instance, virtue, art, music, dancing, reason, spirituality—anything whatever that is transfiguring, refined, foolish, or divine.[12]

Sabbath calls us to return week after week. It is in this act of return that we submit to a simpler way of being. Our obedience in choosing to keep the Sabbath will return us to that which is important. What matters to our souls. It will allow us to re-member that which is at the core of a life well lived.

Tending Your Sabbath Soul

1. How do the concepts of simplicity and Sabbath mind resonate with you at this moment in your life? What would the gifts of Sabbath mind bring to your life and work?

2. As you look at your life, what must you release in order to surrender to a day of Sabbath?

3. What stands in the way, or causes resistance within you, when you consider setting aside twenty-four hours each week for Sabbath?

4. Consider Moishe Konigsberg's statement, "When we cease interfering in the world, we are acknowledging that it is God's world." What does this spark in you in regard to your own life?

2

WHAT MAKES YOUR HEART SING?

The Music of Meaning

After silence, that which comes nearest to expressing the inexpressible is music.
—ALDOUS HUXLEY, "The Rest Is Silence"

OPENING THE HEART

The small Mennonite church in the community of my girlhood was the religious and social hub of the town. It formed and shaped me. Scripture. Community. Service. It was a foundational institution for entraining within me the godly message, the stories of Jesus, of collective and personal spiritual practice, of civic responsibility. As a spiritually sensitive child, I loved the church. It was an oasis amidst the confusion of childhood. Seasons, programs, and people steadied and enriched my small life through music, worship, Sunday school, and youth outings.

As my childhood congregation grew, the place in which I was baptized changed. Increased numbers and giving allowed the worship space to become more than a simple frame country church. New funding birthed an extra balcony, more annexes, a larger sanctuary with a stage, a new heating and cooling system.

No longer were the stained-glass windows flung open on warm summery Sunday mornings to invite in the cool dewy breezes and call of the meadowlark. I missed the outdoor world, the mingling of the grand music of Bach from the pipe organ with creation's song of all living things praising God. Yet as we began to sing four-part hymns, the songs always broke me open to the Creator. Their poetic words would reveal the God of Abraham and Sarah, of Menno Simons and the faith of my grandmothers and grandfathers. The church gifted me the treasure of music—from the church choirs, four-part hymnody, and the beautiful poetry of some of those early hymn writers. I associated Sabbath keeping with singing, literally.

The words of early twentieth-century hymn writer Frederick Lehman make my heart soar as my diaphragm, breath, and bone expand to sing the tune "O Love of God." I can still hear the ordinary saints of that small-town church set among the cornfields, their voices rising together in harmonious concert on a Sunday morning. It is a visceral memory.

> When hoary time shall pass away,
> And earthly thrones and kingdoms fall,
> When men who here refuse to pray,
> On rocks and hills and mountains call,
> God's love so sure, shall still endure,
> All measureless and strong;
> Redeeming grace to Adam's race—
> The saints' and angels' song.
>
> Could we with ink the ocean fill
> And were the skies of parchment made,
> Were every stalk on earth a quill,
> And every man a scribe by trade;
> To write the love of God above

Would drain the ocean dry;
Nor could the scroll contain the whole
Though stretched from sky to sky.

Oh, love of God, how rich and pure!
How measureless and strong!
It shall forevermore endure—
The saints' and angels' song.[1]

For me, music is about being fully alive in the present moment. When one is immersed in singing, the whole body is brought into "now." In that moment the trials and tribulations of daily life fall away. From employing the vibration of sound and breath to fine-tuning multitudes of languages, rhythms, and tempos simultaneously, the human being must stay attuned to what is, not the past or future. Singing is a contemplative act. Making music, much like Sabbath keeping, is an act that transports us from a distracted monkey mind to a full-bodied presence in the moment.

Making music is also a communal act. In any assembled religious ceremony, singing is an activity that engages every age and every voice, without judgment or competition. As the children's song of praise goes, "All God's creatures got a place in the choir." When we leave our daily work to sing in community, we come to the land of our forgotten divine nature. Together we co-create with each other and with God. When a whole choir, a congregation in worship, or an orchestra makes music together, something shifts. Celestial spheres open up and heaven descends. Music has been known as the language of the angelic beings— whether we see them or not. More meaningful than just a passing pop-culture fad or spectator sport of music celebrity stars, congregational singing or groups of people singing have the possibility to invoke the full-bodied Sacred. Perhaps this is because the collective body of humanity comes together in a beautiful and harmonized moment of shalom.

Led by my earliest experiences and love of the church, I eventually followed my heart into the seminary and the congregational ministry track. My work and the people I accompanied brought me into some of the most intimate places of the human condition. Yet I had set aside something inside myself to serve the needs of my people. Much like the church that closed its windows to creation for the sake of "improvement," I had shut out what made my heart sing. Literally, I had stopped singing. I had always studied voice, soloed, and sung in community choirs, quartets, and ensembles as a young woman. Now, except for making a joyful noise with my congregation on Sunday morning, I had quit cold turkey. I didn't want to overshadow my good work with all that performance stuff. Being in the pulpit and up front every Sunday morning was enough. I already chafed against this uncomfortable spotlight that left no place to hide. No need to leave my congregants with the impression that I was hungering for even more attention. I had been taught to mute anything that shone too brightly. It was a safeguard against self-serving narcissism. Congregational singing for worship was highly acceptable. Singing for one's own purposes or for pure pleasure was suspect somewhere in my marrow. I also felt the pinch of time and the overwhelm of duties calling. I figured the best way forward was just to run faster on the treadmill. There was not enough time for music making.

Nurturing our heartsong in alignment with our divine purpose is not something we necessarily learn side by side with potty training. As I suspect happened in my own life, it actually gets unlearned in us over time. I remember the earliest voices shaping me to be wise, economically practical, and efficient with time. Along with everyone else, I was willing to stay in the salt mines, face pointed toward a retirement package, holding my breath until released—*thank God Almighty, free at last*. This is not inherently a bad thing. My Swiss Mennonite and German people have abided by these things for centuries and have succeeded well in this land of the immigrant. This lifetime does require prudence, after all. But as I began to notice, the voice of deeper spiritual growth and yearning usually conflicts with the world's wisdom. The heart of the child—the singer, mystic, player, and lover—open eyes and ears of a different ilk. If the heartsong is silenced, something in us dies. For me, Sabbath would be the winding path back to a deepening meaning and purpose in my life—not just doing something because of external pressure, because I "should," or because I'm matching what is around me. The heartsong is a call to soar, even with my feet firmly planted on terra firma.

THE SONG OF MEANING AND PURPOSE

We spend myriad hours every day doing things to make money, to care for our physical well-being and the well-being of those we love, to accomplish external scheduled duties and demands. We have been taught well to do the things that are efficient and profit-able. We have been well trained not to slow down long enough to listen to the music of our heart. Doing so makes us feel guilty. Or anxious. We might worry about being narcissistic and self-serving. But there comes a time when we realize that what we are doing is at odds with our very God-given essence. Or it all becomes meaningless. Sabbath keeping can give us space to reconnect with our heartsong, to listen to its stirrings and see where it intersects with our work in the world. As spiritual teacher Christine Valters Paintner explains, when we connect with our heart, we go to the place where we can engage our thoughts and emotions in the present moment, the very place where the Sacred resides:

> The heart is an ancient metaphor for the seat of our whole being. To be "whole-hearted" means to bring our

entire selves before God—our intellect, our emotional life, our dreams and intuitions, and our deepest longings. The heart is both active and receptive. The heart listens, but also hears; the heart savors and supplies nourishment to be savored; the heart responds but is also open to the call of others.[2]

Sabbath keeping is more than just a holy day set aside. It is a way of being that can help us reclaim what has been lost. Taking time for Sabbath keeping can take you to the brink of what will make your heart sing, but it is up to you to enter fully, with your heart open, ready for the adventure it may take you on. Little time is made in our life anymore to consider what makes our heart sing, let alone go out and do it. In *Wishful Thinking: A Theological ABC*, American writer and theologian Frederick Buechner writes, "The place God calls you to is the place where your deep gladness and the world's deep hunger meet."[3]

Psychiatrist and Holocaust survivor Viktor Frankl believed that the quest to find meaning in one's life, rather than power and pleasure, is the single most motivating and driving force for humanity. What makes our heart sing is another name for meaning and purpose. Frankl developed logotherapy, a form of psychotherapy, as a way for people to define this in their lives. The basic principles of logotherapy are:

Life has meaning under all circumstances, even the most miserable ones.

Our main motivation for living is our will to find meaning in life.

We have freedom to find meaning in what we do and what we experience, or at least in the stand we take when faced with a situation of unchangeable suffering.[4]

The term *logotherapy* comes from the Greek word *logos*, which has been defined as the divine utterance or communication. In the Christian Gospel of John, it is the Word of God coming into human form. As humans, the urge to communicate what is important and the ability and agency to act has long driven us. We have a deep need for meaning and purpose in our life. Without this, we lose our way. Frankl believed that the anxious individual does not understand that this anxiety is the result of dealing with a sense of "unfulfilled responsibility" and ultimately a lack of meaning.[5]

Meaninglessness is the scourge of our time. It can create the dis-ease of depression and anxiety. In an age of partisan, polarized rage and acrimony in the political sphere, one's own life meaning is erased as we listen to someone else's "spin." As we allow mainstream media to make meaning for us, our heart begins to wither; it goes silent from meanness, and starves in the face of this artificial substitute for our own heartsong. We become mirrors of a shallow society, which doesn't necessarily reflect back what our heart hungers for. Instead, a patchwork quilt of sound bites from someone else's mind and lips populates our mind. The virtual world becomes more real than reality itself. I happen to like Facebook and most social media. But I am aware how easily it can eat up the minutes and hours of my days. Though it makes me laugh at times and I enjoy seeing what is happening in the lives of my friends and family, I know that it is a device of distraction for me. Mind candy. And candy, as I learned as a child, leads to poor health. My soul becomes hungry when this is my steady diet. Sabbath calls me to a media fast. It demands that I decolonize my mind of the fixating virtual space and reality TV culture submerging us.

I found out that a dedicated Sabbath day created breathing space to slow down and listen. Something could begin to shift. My arid heart could become reconstituted when given the time and space to notice what is truly important in my life. It opened up like a flower in bloom. This space for all of us can become a place to return weekly and indulge in that which we long for in our earthly existence—the presence of the Holy. It is what will make our heart truly sing again.

ENTERING THE HEART'S MYSTERY OF MYSTERIES

As I sought to become professionally capable and proficient, focusing fully on my work, I found myself becoming overly serious. I had left a decade of living in the Bay Area, exploring theater, music, dance. Now I had succumbed to a dearth of fun, play, and song because I somehow thought this was a natural casualty of climbing the ladder of success. But at some point along the way, because music had been such an integral part of my life, it dawned on me that music might be the language that could connect me with my work *and* my own heartsong. So I began to check around for avenues for singing. On a whim I tried out for a marvelous community ensemble, Quintessence. During the audition I was terrified but hopeful, and I was ecstatic when I was accepted. We practiced every Sunday night. After a full day of pastoral work, I sometimes had to drag myself, my body exhausted, to rehearsal. But little by little, my heart began to sing her Sabbath song again—connecting me to the rich and songful Sundays of my youth.

A casualty of any profession is the distance we begin to put between our adult world and the enthusiasms that filled our child heart. We rarely return to the great mystery of mysteries at the seat of our being. The Sufis talk about this inner sanctuary where the mysteries of our heart reside. It is there that we restore our knowledge of our true self. Rumi implores us to pay attention to this sacred essence: "You are a ruby in the midst of granite! How long will you continue to deceive us?"[6] We are hardened by the fast track to become competent, well paid, and successful. For ministers this upward ladder can be even more of a hazard. Even as we speak to our congregations about the humble heart as the place where God resides, we are also teaching them about the world of religious constructs and institutional dogmas and scriptures. The dogma can crowd out the idea of a lived heart encounter with the Holy. Mysticism is direct *experience* of the Holy—not intellectual conversation *about* this ineffable Presence. The mystic calls us to go inward to the temple of our heart, where love and hate, and unlovedness and belovedness, lie. Called to explore these inner treasures, we can rid ourselves of the dross and keep the gold. As Frederick Buechner advises:

> Listen to your life. See it for the fathomless mystery it is. In the boredom and pain of it, no less than in the excitement and gladness: touch, taste, smell your way to the holy and hidden heart of it, because in the last analysis all moments are key moments, and life itself is grace.[7]

When I returned to Sabbath keeping—on my chosen day of Monday—the practice opened up a tiny window for my soul to begin to explore my childhood loves. I put a message on my phone. My congregation began to honor and even protect this day for their pastor. Some were interested in studying more about Sabbath keeping. "Like a path through the forest," spiritual teacher Wayne Muller says, "Sabbath creates a marker for ourselves so, if we are lost, we can find our way back to our center."[8]

The great English poet William Blake (1757–1827) writes:

> To see a world in a grain of sand
> and a heaven in a wild flower,
> hold infinity in the palm of your hand
> and eternity in an hour.[9]

A soul spaciousness, a sense of timelessness, can only begin to take hold when we have stopped what we are doing, ceased our labors, and seized upon the divine invitation to come home to our soul—what Buechner describes as the "original, shimmering self [that] gets buried so deep that most of us end up hardly living out of it at all. Instead we live out all the other selves, which we are constantly putting on and taking off like coats and hats against the world's weather."[10] Sabbath keeping is the invitation to reenter that holy mystery of mysteries, the landscape of our heart. My Monday Sabbaths began to seed this eternity inside of me. It was the time and quietude I needed to plumb the depths of that which had been lost for so long—what had grown cold inside of me.

THE SWEET RESURRECTION
OF THE HEARTSONG

Eventually Sabbath time and my reconnection with nature's rhythm revived in me another heartsong. This one about the humble honeybee. One day I received a visitation from wild honeybees who were living in our neighbor's air duct. The bees fascinated me, possessing more and more of my imagination. I longed to become a beekeeper. So I did. Little did I know they were sent to me to help resurrect my heartsong, which had become overly cultivated and too heady.

Honeybees are an ancient symbol of resurrection and new life, showing up in a noblewoman's tomb over five thousand years ago.[11] In the great Easter Vigil of the Catholic Church, on the Saturday night before Easter when the faithful gather to anticipate the resurrection, the Exsultet is sung. Written in the fourth or fifth century, this joyful song that welcomes the risen Christ features the humble honeybee and the beauty of her life-giving gifts from the hive. Benedictine beekeeper Brother Nick Kleespie writes, "The second section of the Exsultet is the praise of the candle [which] proclaims the Paschal mystery that this night the darkness of sin is destroyed and the faithful are restored to grace."[12] The bees became an integral part of the celebration through their contribution of the candle's beeswax.

On this, your night of grace, O holy Father,
accept this candle, a solemn offering,
the work of bees and of your servants' hands,
an evening sacrifice of praise,
this gift from your most holy Church.

But now we know the praises of this pillar,
which glowing fire ignites for God's honor,
a fire into many flames divided,
yet never dimmed by sharing of its light,
for it is fed by melting wax,
drawn out by mother bees
to build a torch so precious.[13]

As I have come to learn, Sabbath keeping and beekeeping have much in common. When I put on my veil and enter the inner sanctum of the honeybee hive, into the realm of tens of thousands of humming wings, I am transported. Bees throughout history have been deeply connected to our human story. Aside from the legendary elixir of honey, bee's complex social societies have also fascinated humans. In many ways they show us the best of who we can be as humans, working together for a common cause and the good of all. Time is always suspended when I enter the hive. New mysteries of my own heart are revealed to me. In my relationship with the bees, as in my relationship with Sabbath keeping, I come face-to-face with a whole rash of life's mysteries: grace, beauty, awe, death, forgiveness, mercy, and kindness. One of my favorite poems is by Spanish poet Antonio Machado:

Last night as I was sleeping,
I dreamt—marvelous error!—
that I had a beehive
here inside my heart.
And the golden bees
were making white combs
and sweet honey
from my old failures.

Last night as I was sleeping,
I dreamt—marvelous error!—
that a fiery sun was giving
light inside my heart.
It was fiery because I felt
warmth as from a hearth,
and sun because it gave light
and brought tears to my eyes.

Last night as I slept,
I dreamt—marvelous error!—
that it was God I had
here inside my heart.[14]

Much like the gift of Sabbath and music making, the time spent working in the hive is soul time. It's like that when you love something or someone. Your heartstrings thrum with joy when you are in the presence of this thing, this being that makes your heart sing. As a beekeeper, when I stand in the middle of my beehives in the morning, surrounded by the busy buzz of hundreds of thousands of bees flying in and out of their hive, I feel the marvelous hum of life itself.

HEARTSONG HOMECOMING

As I embarked on my Sabbath Mondays, they took me on a winding inward journey to rediscover my passions and reignite my tired soul. As I gathered at St. John's United Methodist Church every Sunday night to practice with my other choral mates, I noticed that everyone else also came from busy lives—teaching, law, medicine, business, ministry, parenting, studying. I noticed the dedication and appetite to sing that animated those who showed up week after week. Our director, Matt, fed us a rich diet of sacred and contemporary, rollicking, playful, jazzy, and somber songs of many traditions—from Bach to Navajo to African American. Though I was physically spent, I felt myself vibrating with joy after three hours of singing. Ready and relaxed for a peaceful slumber. This weekly rhythm created a threshold to Monday Sabbath at sundown. I began to hear soul stirrings with the ear of my heart and contemplate new directions at this midlife juncture. As I reconnected to singing again, I was reorienting my spiritual compass. Both music and Sabbath became oracles and guides as I entered the wilderness of a middle-age crisis.

Like the devotee's act of singing in worship, whether Hindu, Christian, Muslim, or Jewish, singing enlivens the ears of one's heart and prepares the community to hear the stirrings of the soul. For me as a Mennonite, worship always featured four-part hymnody; a place of singular voice, healing, wholeness, and renewal. It had a way of focusing unity in mind, body, and soul, of opening the heart. During the sixteenth-century Reformation, Anabaptists (the ancestors of the Mennonites and Amish) sang as they were lashed to stakes and burned for their beliefs. Eventually the torturers learned to cut out their tongues or bolt them down, trying to silence their joyous testimonies. "In Thee Is Gladness," a song that congregations still sing today, came from the repertoire of the martyrs. It came from a people whose souls were undaunted by fear, lifted up by their collective song.

For monasteries and convents, chant or plainsong has been a staple of worship life together. A calling of the faithful home to the house where God lives. Singing the Psalms comes from centuries of fine-tuning the Liturgy of the Hours. Broken open to the public somewhere in the last century, monastic communities made popular recordings of their prayerful chants—the rich male timbre distinct and calming, the soaring female voices enunciating German Abbess Hildegard of Bingen's compositions from the eleventh century. For an increasingly liturgically deafened and spiritually asleep population, the monastery was now available to the secular world. I still remember the cover of a CD with stylized monks on the cover and the title *Chant* splashed across the top in the 1990s. Men's voices in one accord were somewhat sexy and cool for a young Mennonite woman. Oddly enough I would find the Liturgy of the Hours a direct route to my own devotional practice years later—the sung Psalms bringing me home in a way.

For African American slaves, singing was a buffer against the challenges and disappointments of tyranny, a touchstone of solidarity. It bound them together and lifted their heads toward glory land and, eventually, justice. In all places and all times, people have stretched beyond their limited imaginations and yoked themselves to extraordinary actions and unexpected new directions in their short life spans, with the body of their collective tunes and the songs of their heart guiding them. As Jewish singer-songwriter Joey Weisenberg explains:

> Music teaches us how to listen—if we let it. It is through careful listening that we learn how to get "in tune" with the people, spaces, and spiritual energies around us. . . . It is through intentional listening, our tradition teaches,

that we are able to close our eyes and better hear the unity that underlies all of creation. . . . When our hearts are opened through music, we are more vulnerable, but we are also more receptive to insight.[15]

It is as though we are listening with the ear of our heart, in a place of intuition, understanding, and joy.

As music began to peel me open again, I longed for more time to listen to my inner guidance with the ear of my heart. During my extended Sabbath visit to the Benedictine monks of Christ in the Desert, one late afternoon in June I came upon Wednesday Vespers. That day the sung prayers were dedicated to the sacred heart of Jesus, and I had gone early for the silent prayer with the Blessed Sacrament, made visible for this special day. I noticed the heaviness of the air at that time of the afternoon, the sun's thick golden liquid drawing across the canyon floor. I heard the locusts buzzing in the distance. From my wooden pew, my spine facing the doors flung open on that hot afternoon, I daydreamed of the thick, sultry August days of my childhood on the family farm. Summer almost gone and the fields cut to stubble, hay drying with a sweet fragrance that clung to the moist air. I saw myself as the little girl who sat enthralled in the Sunday morning pew of the frame church of my youth, the summer morning pouring through the open windows.

My attention returned to the Benedictine chapel. The silent visitation was over; the monks were filing in for the sung Vespers. The monk's lives were a shrouded mystery to me except for this visible worship that the casual visitor was invited to attend. This time of common chant revealed a small glimpse into their humanness. I wondered if they, like ordinary seekers such as myself, also found these Sabbath moments challenging to keep. Endearing to me was the young monk who always knelt over by the screen on the front left of the altar. It was as though he was crumpled and could not arise. He knelt there throughout the whole twenty minutes. I wondered if he was sleeping.

As I sat in the back pew, I felt the sweat gather on my back, even in my airy cotton blouse. I loved these adobe buildings and the fact that there was no air conditioning whatsoever. The thick walls cooled and warmed the church, regulating the outside air. I thought of our amazing bodies—our fluid pumping against skin, regulating constant temperature. They worked in much the same way as the mud of the adobe. We are soil and water after all.

As we chanted the age-old texts together, the words wove themselves around my body, stretching out to link me with the earth elements all around me. As the soothing yet powerful sound circled around me, my inner vision flew to the top of the chapel, my eyes catching the red cliffs again in the late afternoon sun. The music soared and climaxed; it collided with the smells, sounds, and textures. Taking off my shoes, I felt the cool floor against my feet as I stood, my kneeling pad before me. It was a full-bodied and extravagant Sabbath keeping. My heart was home. In that moment I rested in the sacred heart of Jesus, filled with the flame of love.

As new chords were woven into my soul, I wondered what other Sabbath gems would show up to companion me. Perhaps rekindling my relationship with nature? She had always been a place of solace and joy during every period of my life. My heart-song had been enlivened in nature as well. I could trust my heart, opening like a rose, to lead me on new adventures as I set aside Sabbath space each week to show up.

Tending Your Sabbath Soul

1. What made your heart sing as a child? How are you still connected to this child delight as an adult?

2. Describe the ways that your life pulls you away from your heartsong and the Sabbath that can restore it.

3. Share a story of a time when you have ceased your labors, allowing yourself to remember your heartsong.

4. Psychiatrist and Holocaust survivor Viktor Frankl believed that the quest to find meaning in one's life, rather than having power and pleasure, is the single most motivating and driving force for humanity. What has given your life its deepest meaning?

5. Music can be a path to the place that the Sabbath Mystery of Mysteries, the Holy of Holies, resides. What place does music have in your life?

3

CREATION AS
SABBATH COMPANION
Divine Presence Everywhere

Ours is a mysterious universe and we are asked
to awaken to the preciousness of divine Presence
in every moment. "If a drop of the wine of vision
could rinse our eyes," says our friend Rumi,
"everywhere we look we would weep with wonder."
—JAMAL RAHMAN, *Spiritual Gems of Islam*

CREATION'S GENEROSITY

I had been in the saddle for a very long time. Ministry was holy
work and I loved my chosen vocation, but with the relentless
cycle of weekly worship and preaching alongside the increasing
demands of a growing congregation, Monday Sabbath was no
longer enough. Even the vacation days spread out across the year
did not meet the requirements of an overstretched soul. My colleagues petitioned me to take an extended Sabbath—a sabbatical.
I felt timid about talking with my congregation about taking one.
They worked year round without sabbaticals. Why should I be
different? But I knew that ministry was a 24/7 job. Even when I
wasn't "on," my mind was picking through the events of the day

or the upcoming sermon, which came like clockwork every week. I read that pastor and writer Eugene Peterson had negotiated an annual extended Sabbath with his congregation. He and his family would live at their family cabin in Montana each summer. It was a way of revitalizing his ministry and spending time with his beloveds—and living close to the land. After seven years I knew I needed something like that. Wishing I had been mentored early on in these ways of caring for myself in the midst of active ministry, I could see how extended periods of Sabbath might sustain a ministry for a lifetime. So I applied for a grant to go and was given the green light. It would be the first of two. I went into the heart of nature. She was a good companion.

I began my first sabbatical by spending four days at a lake cottage, thanks to the generosity of my brother and his wife. It was a time to reconstitute my weary traveling bones. The first thing I did when I awakened that first day was try to call my bank and find out how much was left in my checking account. The cell phone signal was poor. As I spoke to the electronic teller, it dropped my voice-activated requests over and over. Finding myself becoming frustrated and irritated, I began to shout into the phone. Out on the wooden deck with birds beginning their morning praise song, I furtively glanced around at the homes next door in these woods. Suddenly I was silenced by embarrassment. My anxiety over finances was laughable out here. What could I do anyway, on a Sunday morning with a bad mobile connection, by a lake in the middle of the midwestern cornfields? What did I think—that somehow I could control my fortunes from here? That I was in danger of losing my daily bread? I smiled. Everything I needed was right there, in that moment.

Hanging up, I reoriented my priorities for the morning. It would be a Sabbath day. I noticed that down on the dock, walking along the wooden slats in its funny long-toed galoshes, was the prehistoric-looking blue heron. This one had been carefully checking out the water. She jumped in for a better look at the minnows. When she heard me stir, she stopped. Stock still, she cocked her head for what seemed like an eternity. I became motionless. Her livelihood came from the daily generosity of this lake ecosystem. She did not worry where her next meal would come from. Her instinct drove her to find her daily bread, if only she showed up and waited. Patiently, she treaded those waters day after day, rain or shine.

I lugged my kayak down to the shoreline and dumped it into the lake. The heron gracefully took flight, her wingspan like a small plane. I watched her land on the opposite shore and continue her careful sifting. My paddle cut the glassy surface of the lake, and I steered my boat for a while, until I began to drift toward the opposite shoreline. I saw a pair of kingfishers, testily flying ahead of me, peering at me from under their leafy domes. I was startled by a very large fish angling out of the water in front of me, splashing and then returning to the depths of the green-brown waters. Oak and maple, cherry, willow, tulip, locust, and hickory hardwoods paraded along the shore, mirrored in the lake. Mist rose around me, and I trailed my fingers in the warm waters, settling back into the kayak. I was enjoying the morning, devoid of human voices and activity. The creatures were welcome companions, my silent reverie punctuated by the morning sounds of this lakeside community of birds and fish, water, wind, and sunlight.

My preoccupation with my bank account and money began to fade away and I thought of Jesus's teaching, "Do not worry about your life, what you will eat or drink; or about your body, what you will wear. . . . Look at the birds of the air; they do not sow or reap or store away in barns, and yet your heavenly Father feeds them. Are you not more valuable than they?" (Matthew 6:25–26). What seemed like a radical teaching in first-century agrarian Palestine began to make sense. That living lake community was bound together in a plenitude of generosity and reciprocity. My task that day was to pay attention to this cycle of nature's generosity, to link my own abundance with this rather than disregard it. As I released my anxiety and obsessiveness over my paltry material possessions, I realized that my wealth was much larger than my participation in human economies. It was not measured in dollars, retirement portfolios, and stuff I owned.

As I opened the room of my heart to nature, she responded generously, in kind. I began to notice the golden eagle who paid a visit in the morning, sitting confidently in a relaxed manner on the dead branch outside my bedroom window. I heard the mating cardinal pair with their multitudinous refrains, saw their darting red movement in the thick leafy branches. The shy, reclusive wren, who came to peek at me from the hedge around the deck, so silent that I would have missed her if I hadn't been sitting without movement for over an hour. The gifts of nature are immense.

I was reminded of the woman with the alabaster jar. In the synoptic Gospels, this woman, whether Mary of Bethany, Jesus's friend, or the oft-maligned loose woman whom some have called Mary Magdalene, extravagantly poured pure nard over her beloved Jesus. She anointed him with her hair and tears. It was an outrageous act of sheer trust, love, and abundance, with no utilitarian purpose whatsoever. No regard for propriety. No thought of the future. She broke all the rules of human economy at that time, as she generously dispensed of a year's worth of wages.

If there is any bug, bird, bat, or mammal that offers us such Sabbath generosity, honeybees take the cake. Every element from the hive—honey, pollen, propolis, royal jelly—is of extravagant value for health, vigor, and healing of many ailments. Bees populate the enchanted world of flowers, beauty, and living things, making the miraculous elixir of honey as they buzz and pollinate, vibrating at speeds that fascinate the observer. They come from a mythical, mysterious, otherworldly place of nonverbal wisdom. It is a place that most are miserably inept at understanding, lacking even a desire to know. But children are different. The creaturely and invisible world has not yet been socialized out of them. They are still attuned to this nonhuman reality.

Sabbath keeping is like that bee space. I became a beekeeper in those busy years of ministry, and these tiny invertebrates often became my Sabbath companions, teaching me about generosity. If my ministry called me to a verbal, structured, professional world of competence, the bees called me to leave this for the uncharted places of nature—a space that required me to learn with a beginner's mind.

Seeing through the eyes of a bee, or listening with the ears of a creature, taught me what it was to love the heart of the humble poor—the wordless and voiceless—of which creation was among the most vulnerable. The bee space became an oasis of reciprocity, of the generosity of the creaturely world, so easily missed in a society moving at breakneck speed. When I truly wanted or needed to enter Sabbath mind, I could go to the hive. If I entered slowly, with contemplative mindfulness, following the procedures that honor one's coming—sending a smoke signal, moving slowly, not harming or squashing their sisters (yes, all the bee workers are female), doing one's business quickly and with increasing skill—I was allowed entry unharmed. A generous act, as I came unbidden into their inner sanctum where all intimate life happens. When I was rushed, anxious, uncertain, and did not take the time to follow the guidelines that honored my bees, they mirrored back to me my own interior landscape—with less than pleasant consequences. I came to know that bees are terribly forgiving when it comes to my raw mistakes wrecking their home and creating more work for them—a dropped tool, a melted honeycomb, crushed brood and worker. Yet every time we would start with a clean slate. They drew me into Sabbath time. Slowing me down and asking me to honor their work and lives.

The quintessential generosity of the earth can only be experienced by taking Sabbath time to sit within her and notice such immense and free gifts

THE SLOW HEARTBEAT OF CREATION

I found that nature was a wonderful Sabbath companion. But in order for her to accompany me, it required that I unplug from technology, which, if it's not a newly labeled addiction in the current edition of the *Diagnostic and Statistical Manual of Mental Disorders*, the psychology bible, I wondered if it should be. Going into creation required a slower pace, asking for all five senses, as well as intuition, that spiritual sensibility, to be alive and attuned. Leaving behind devices and all the ways I was constantly wired into our society was not easy. Pastor and author Wayne Muller writes:

> When we live without listening to the timing of things—when we live and work in twenty-four-hour shifts without rest—we are on war time, mobilized for battle. Yes, we are strong and capable people, we can work without stopping, faster and faster, electric lights making artificial day so the whole machine can labor without ceasing. But remember: *No living thing lives like this.* There are greater rhythms that govern how life grows: circadian rhythms, seasons and hormonal cycles and sunsets and moonrises and great movements of seas and stars. We are part of the creation story, subject to all its laws and rhythms.[1]

Our crazed lives and tightly wound human schedules give us an exaggerated sense of self-importance. For me, Sabbath keeping was about being freed from the false idea that I was indispensable.

In this freedom, my true life—which often became submerged and swept under the rug—could unfold as I took time set apart. I found creation to be a humble and constant companion. Her slow heartbeat brought me to my senses. Given time and attention, the sweet spaces of nature opened doors within me.

A "thin place" that changed and healed me during my first sabbatical was the Scottish islands of Mull and Iona. My journey began in Mull. I was slated to stay in an old quarry workers' outpost that had been refurbished by the Presbyterian Church of Scotland. This was before the onslaught of wireless and cell phones. I happily unplugged from my computer to live on this rugged, wind-whipped island for a week. Here, people from all walks of life, young and old, drew close to the slow heartbeat of nature for Sabbath rest. I knew that the quarters would be rustic, fueled only by wind power and fire, but I had no idea that the block buildings where we slept in stacks of bunk beds would be without heat. Every night, decked out in layers of clothing, we would enter the icy tombs, quickly slipping between the covers. The only place where we could stay warm when standing upright was by the peat-moss fire in the main eating area. In the early morning light, we raced through our morning ablutions to join each other in the cheerful kitchen for tea.

Our guide for the week was a Celtic theologian and pastor. It was in her company that I began to understand nature as the first revelation of God. The Celtic Christians called nature the "Big Book" of God's revelation. For them, this preceded the scriptures written down by human pen. God was first revealed and experienced in the firmament, the creatures, the waters, and the soil. The biblical story and imagination was birthed out of creation's genesis. The "Little Book," the scriptures of the people of God, then followed as the written narrative. The book of Genesis laid out the ordered blueprint of this original vision of the Big Book of creation.

In the first century, the apostle Paul was writing a letter to the Roman Jewish Christians—people bound up by an empire that dominated antiquity. He wrote:

> For since the creation of the world God's invisible qualities—his eternal power and divine nature—have been clearly seen, being understood from what has been made, so that people are without excuse. (Romans 1:20)

He reminded the people that the God of heaven was plainly seen in the created order around them. It was this creation that revealed truth—the correct path to walk. Saint Paul preached that the waywardness of the surrounding culture was foolish and futile. The revelation of God in and through creation called the faithful to lives rightly aligned with such a magnificent presence.

During our time on Mull, we scrambled through bogs and hiked toward the sea, hugging brambly bushed, muddy trails. We examined delicate flowers as our guide read us Psalms to inspire our imaginations. We kayaked in the swirling open waters that sucked at the cliffs around us. We laughed at the herd of sheep, clustering close to the stone house where we stayed, staring googly-eyed at us. We gathered every night around the long table by the peat fire to swap stories, hear the history of the isles, and warm our toes. I learned that the Celtic Christians believed the Mystery of Mysteries resides in the fragile resilience of the human pulse and creation's beating heart, side by side. Humans, creatures, and plant life all nestled together in the great heart of God, hungering to be resurrected from the oppression of ceaseless labor.

The primitive rhythm of Sabbath rest, slowing and stopping, grew in me as I lived on this island of the Celts. It was there waiting for me under layers and layers of civilized time. It was nature's restful beat. In my mind, I traced the roots of my own godly introduction to this Big Book of creation. On the particular plot of farmland where I was sewn as a child, I walked the cow trails with my dog, a sense of place rooting my whole being in that good soil. My brothers and I spent feral summers exploring every hedgerow, forest, creek, and cow trail. Nature was a place of rest, creativity, respite, and healing for me. I would take leave from my chores and the dynamics of our household, escaping to those first stirrings of God in the nonverbal world of creatures and creation—a place where God would speak subtly, without distraction. It was my Sabbath time as a child, though the word "Sabbath" was largely unbeknownst to me, except as the day we went to church as a family.

My earliest memories of encountering the Real, the Presence that dwelt in my soul, were in the natural world, not the halls of doctrine making. My spiritual life and identity as a young girl was formed and shaped as much by that landscape as by the Mennonite church. With creation as my companion, I opened myself wholeheartedly to God. I came home to the infinitude in my own soul, walking in solitude, spinning stories, and singing songs that I made up. Nature was intimate companion and elder grandmother, walking alongside with her wisdom ways. Here I emptied out from the hurts of childhood, releasing the confusion of wounds from an adult world. Time stood still. It allowed me to listen to my own soul, not just the words of human culture that sometimes left me confused and overwhelmed. These were the sacred moments that filled me with what I've come to know as Sabbath mind—that slow heartbeat that infuses creation. Nature is spacious, operating in a different time than our usual busy, measured wristwatch *chronos* time, which traps us in a very small place. Birds praise. Creatures live slow, deliberate lives. Trees take years, even decades, to grow into their full stature. The plants and waters take billions of years to evolve into their wisdom.

As I left the Isle of Mull, the thunderclouds in me were beginning to gather. The empty spaciousness of the week had turned up an old memory. Grief washed up on the shores of my consciousness, and I could no longer ignore it. I could feel myself becoming shipwrecked by my emotions. In her pastoral perception, our leader noted my increasing silence and brooding. She invited me to talk with her as needed. I could only withdraw deeper into myself, ashamed, burdened by guilt and sorrow.

The day came to board the ferry to the Isle of Iona. Creation conspired to walk with me even in my darkest hour. The skies cut loose and sheets of rain pummeled the boat. It was impossible to see the jewels of the islands as one could on a clear day. It didn't matter. I had no heart for it. The people on board clung to the coffee shop and dry halls inside the boat. Then a voice within called me to stand at the railing as the rain receded, leaving only a very wet mist to enshroud me as I stood there. Suddenly, my face and coat drenched in moisture, it was as though a divine portal had opened up. In my abandonment, I heard a voice: *I have been with you at every moment of your life, though you have not known it. You are beloved.* Twenty minutes I stood there, bathed in this knowing. It felt like an eternity. Forgiveness rained down on me. Abraham Joshua Heschel describes Sabbath time spent aimlessly as the grandeur and glory of eternal time. Now I knew it in my bones. Something had lifted in that infinite moment. I felt lighter.

I returned to my ministry and continued with Sabbath Mondays. Remembering my time on the boat to Iona, I allowed nature to beckon me. If I wanted to fill myself with God, I would head down to the river or up to the mountains. There I shed calloused layers of thick armor in which I wrapped myself. Fresh as a newborn, I began to feel the sparkle of new ideas and renewed energy rise up. Sabbath became a time to return to the earth, a time to rekindle my passion, my enthusiasms—which my husband reminded me comes from the Greek root *enthousiasmos*, literally meaning "to be filled with God." I was reconnected again and again. Sabbath time in nature was a place of peace and total joy for me. Wendell Berry's epic poem "The Peace of Wild Things" became my rallying cry. Something about participating in the natural world where every living being is acting purely out of its essence and "is-ness" allowed me to relax. Pretension slipped away. Feeling my truer self there than in most of human-constructed reality, creation was my extended family. Soul kin. And as such, my Sabbath keeping would have been impoverished without the times spent in creation. Here I re-membered the whole web of life that I eternally exist within as only one living being among many.[2] Tertullian, a third-century Father of the Church and often called the first Christian theologian, said "enfleshment is the hinge of salvation."[3] Building on this, Franciscan Richard Rohr noted that the world itself is the primary locus of the sacred, providing all the metaphors that the soul needs to mature:

> We don't come to the God Mystery through concepts or theories but by connecting with *what is*—with God's immediate, embodied presence which is all around us. I want you to begin to notice that almost all of Jesus' common stories and examples are nature based and relationship based—and never once academic theory![4]

Like I did before coming home to my soul on the boat to Iona, I continued to need to unplug and show up to nature's slow heartbeat, drawing me closer to my true self. In the midst of the forces of creation, a great healing could begin. The Iona Celtic cross around my neck continued to remind me of creation as Sabbath's companion. A circle of creation's life with the cross at the center. The axis mundi of the earth connecting heaven and earth. Life and death. Death and Resurrection.

BEAUTY AS NATURE'S SABBATH SIREN

The poet Mary Oliver said in a talk at Wellesley College, "Beauty gives us an ache, to be worthy of [it]."[5] New fields of creative perspectives and imaginings blossom within us when we take Sabbath time to be in this beauty. The Hebrew and Christian scriptures delight in the world of matter. Beauty abounds in creation. Angels and portents of heaven visit earthlings bound by time and space. Simple things like bushes, rocks, wells, and night skies become illuminated with divine meaning. Relationship between human and earth is all there in that moment, blessed by God. It is the first breath of the child in the manger, with choirs of angels heralding his coming. It is the lilies of the field, the sparrows of the air, the golden grain waving their alluring heads for Jesus and his disciples to eat on the Sabbath. It is the Psalm of David, the firmament declaring God's glory, and the skies as the work of God's hands.

Beauty is necessary to life, second only to water. I am a firm believer of this. There is an enchantment in creation that we can only see if we slow down long enough to notice. Yet day by day we become immune to the beauty that we are ensconced and held within. When we deny ourselves art and creative spaces—more, not less, green space—our collective soul becomes impoverished. It renders us less resilient, less capable of dreaming or living into a new future—our minds colonized by a culture drenched in fear, violence, poverty, and eco-cide. How can we so easily succumb to the lack of beauty as normal? Color. Texture. Sensual smells. Sounds. We miss the most amazing collections of molecules that live next to us—an ant, a flower, a tree.

One summer sabbatical my husband and I climbed up our first twelve-thousand-foot pass. We had come to the Maroon Bells near Aspen, Colorado. I felt like a pack animal, remembering the little Ethiopian donkeys I saw when I visited East Africa.

As cheap horsepower for much of the ancient world and those developing countries today, these donkeys were loaded with six feet of hay fastened firmly on their backs. Their heads down, they patiently plodded forward. All they could see was the path before each hoof they put forward.

Sweating profusely, I tried to imagine my feet stapled to the ground one by one as I walked at what seemed like a ninety-degree angle—straight upward on red scree and broken rocks. It was a ribbon of a path with a sheer drop-off next to my boots. Trying not to imagine vertigo or hyperventilate, my mind wandered to the sharp and treacherous boulder field at the bottom. I heard a pika squeaking his plaintive warning cry over and over. As I glanced behind, there was a village of humans snaking upward to the summit. Though I've always been sure-footed as a mountain goat, I began to question my stability.

Suddenly wildflower fields clothed in a profusion of colors and glorious shapes and sizes manifested before my very eyes. I was being accosted by beauty in this high alpine country. I counted at least four colors of Indian paintbrush alone. Flocks of yellow daisies, purple asters. Clusters of columbine. Seas of indigo bluebells and all manner of column-like flowers, such as lupine. Then there were the bouquets of teeny-tiny pink-and-purple starlets, jumping out at me from cracks in the rock. Like cheerful little faces, they shouted, "Surprise! Surprise!" In this meadow, miles high above and far from the asphalt parking lot, I was overwhelmed by beauty. The teachings of the Sermon on the Mount came to me: "And why do you worry about clothes? See how the flowers of the field grow. They do not labor or spin" (Matthew 6:28).

Remembering a friend long ago, marveling aloud at splendidly textured and colored fish and sea creatures so deep in the ocean that they may never be noticed by the human eye, I smiled. "Imagine a God who creates just for the sheer joy of it!" she cried in her usual childlike exuberance.

The beauty of nature is a respite, a refuge of Sabbath. A place to breathe again. A place to flee to that Shining Presence that is in all, beyond all, and through all. It is an immenseness that we cannot see when our feet are pinned to the urban jungles of our cities. The mystic and Jesuit Teilhard de Chardin (1881–1955) often waded into the beauty of creation as a geologist and theologian:

> Throughout my whole life . . . during every moment I have lived, the world has gradually been taking on a light and fire for me, until it has come to envelop me in one mass of luminosity, glowing from within. . . . This is what I have learnt from my contact with the earth—the diaphany of the Divine at the heart of a glowing universe, the Divine radiating from the depth of matter aflame.[6]

This diaphany, or transparency, of God at the heart of the universe never failed to astound and inspire me when I went into her beauty for Sabbath. Creation was an eternally evolving earth community of utter beauty and intricacy, and it retrained my senses for beauty as I reentered the dance of life in my workaday world.

CREATION'S CALL TO SHABBAT SHALOM

Creation can become a mirror to the things that are untransformed within us when she is our companion. Sabbath days are not always wonderful, lovely walks in the park. They can also become a seedbed of reflection as the separation between earth and self is erased. Here in creation, we can be opened up to moral and ethical questions and dilemmas of our relationship with the natural world. Increasingly, our Western civilization has marginalized and "conquered" nature rather than embraced her as a place to listen, learn, and become an interdependent participant in the dance of creation. In her primordial rhythms, she can make us uncomfortable. It is precisely her wild, untamed, beating heart that can disturb or provoke us, so tirelessly have we tried to stamp out and domesticate these characteristics in ourselves. Practicing Sabbath in the company of the natural world can be a pathway to a new way of thinking and being. As we cease our usual activity, the hidden secrets that we've locked away reveal themselves. Nature can be a stern teacher. Unwavering in her truth. If you are brave enough to wander into her recesses and release control of your life to a mystery larger than yourself, you may just come face-to-face with yourself—a soul unmasked.

As the writer and tireless environmental crusader Edward Abbey knew:

> Wilderness is not a luxury but a necessity of the human spirit, and as vital to our lives as water and good bread. A civilization which destroys what little remains of the wild, the spare, the original, is cutting itself off from its origins and betraying the principle of civilization itself.[7]

Our first day on the sabbatical trail, visiting the Maroon Bells in the Colorado Rockies, two young men approached us. They came down the trail on their way out of the national forest. We were heading deeper, a steady upward spin. My husband struck up a conversation with these men, who looked to be the age of his high school students. When they found out that they all shared the same birthplace and home state of Georgia, rapid-fire questions ensued. "Where did you grow up?" "Oh, do you know . . . ?" "Have you ever been to . . . ?" I was getting lost in the conversation, pretty much packing up the snacks in preparation to go. When my husband asked if they'd seen any wildlife, a look passed between them.

"Well . . . yeah . . . sort of."

"Last night a deer wandered into our campsite. My brother picked up a rock and threw it," the huskier of the two said.

I was back in the conversation. "So you scared it away?" I asked.

Another look passed between the two. The smaller, dark-haired man said somewhat apologetically, now that he saw my attention was riveted, "Well, I hit him really hard in the head, between the eyes. The deer ran."

We were all suddenly silent. My husband jumped in and said something reassuring like, "Probably wasn't that hard. The deer must be okay."

"No. It was *really* hard," the young man reiterated persistently. They both looked uncomfortable now. It was as though they were confessing their act, wanting absolution.

I was suddenly sick to my stomach. I picked up my pack and began walking ahead rather than finish out the conversation with polite amenities. As I struggled with my racing thoughts, I became the deer. Feeling the crack of the rock on my skull, the searing pain startled me into action. I leapt as quickly as I could, away from the thing that issued the pain. I wondered, *Did the deer survive? What would happen in the wild? Would it die alone? Was it mortally wounded and would it stumble for days until hunted down and eaten?*

This act of violence in the middle of this majestic and seemingly idyllic place shattered something inside me, knowing how thin is the thread of survival for creatures in the wild. Life and death—a constant spiral, a sort of roulette. Predator and prey. Harsh weather and uncertain conditions. Summer lasted precious few months and then every ounce of physical and instinctual fiber and wit was needed to live through the winter. If a critter hadn't become ill or old by this time, it might survive one more year. Suffering was a part of daily existence. Introducing humans into the equation made their lives even dicier.

For Hildegard of Bingen (1098–1179), the great Benedictine Doctor of the Church, nature was a mirror for the soul and a mirror for God. She understood humanity as a microcosm of the macrocosm of the universe, embedded in the Creator. Creation was not merely a stage for humans to perform on, but an active agent in human transformation. The outer world was needed to mirror the inner world. When we come to creation as our Sabbath companion to explore the virgin territory within us, she holds a mirror up to our untransformed ideas about the world, others, and ourselves. Hildegard knew this would require a whole new consciousness of human experience and understanding on earth. In her book *Scivias*, she writes, "You understand so little of what is around you because you do not use what is within you."[8]

Creation is intrinsically alive and valuable in and of itself, not just for human consumption, meddling, and manipulation. Sabbath keeping can liberate us from a harsh, utilitarian worldview. As we move into the natural world to find companions there, we can forge a bridge to those whom indigenous people have always known are their relations—nonhuman beings. In a day that is so clearly about giving up our own control, Sabbath asks us to lay down the tools of our trade—computers, language, profit sheets, medical equipment, machines, guns, industry—and begin to build a different world together. One where we become coconspirators with God for a more peaceful planet. A place yearning toward Eden and a peaceable kin-dom with all living beings. Shabbat shalom. Sabbath peace.

GRATITUDE: WAKING UP
FROM OUR AMNESIA

One Sabbath, I was sitting by Snowmass Lake in Colorado, a glacial body of water as ancient as the mountains that surround it. Considering water's properties and the fact that it is recycled for every purpose on earth, I sat in amazement. Such wisdom is held in this diluter, hydrator, refresher, the stuff of life itself. Our very bodies are made up of 70 percent water. We are water babies. Why would we ever wantonly and mindlessly ruin this incredible substance? I wondered. As the Standing Rock Sioux language reminded me, *mni wiconi*, water is life—more closely translated "water is alive." Without it we cannot live. I saw it tumbling down from the rocky peaks around me in flowing waterfalls, filled with innumerable minerals that composed my body and every living thing around me. This landscape, close to the ceiling of the sky, was knit together in a brilliant, seamless garment. All the creatures taking their cues from instincts embedded deep within them; the weather cycles that came and went, setting the whole of this circle spinning and re-creating continually.

That night I listened for hours to the soft rain on our tent. In the morning it had soaked the pine needles and softened the soil, watering the millions of plant fibers and greenery around us. Water restores. Water cleanses. Water is wise. I thought to myself, "If we were conscious, we would fall down on our knees and give thanks every day for water and safeguard her with our lives." I began to make a practice of saying a prayer of gratitude every time I used water to clean, cook, bathe, or drink. Simple gratitude for her gift of life began to awaken me from my amnesia about the exquisite world we live embedded within.

Gratitude became a staple of my Sabbath days. As Judy, a dear friend, wisely said, gratitude is medicinal. With my body full of other people's energy and my mind constipated from a very wordy world of work, I could walk out of my house and away from all my duties with my senses blown wide open to the large and small glories of creation. I'd change tracks from my worka-day world to Sabbath by bathing in gratitude for creation's gifts. Gratitude *was* good medicine. If I was angry, the toxic waste of my thoughts slipped away. If I was grieving a loss, giving thanks for that which was lost opened up my heart to release. If I was frenetic, as I began to give thanks for everything around me, I sank into the slower heartbeat of creation.

Nature today is suffering not only from our amnesia that we share the same root of creation, but also because of an economic system that has run amuck. We are caught up in a dizzying pace that destroys creation in the name of progress, treading upon the home of most creatures, forests, soil communities, and watersheds, mindlessly evicting and displacing other life-forms on the planet, showing utter disregard for how they companion us in every way. If the water is polluted by fracking or privatized for the few, it will exact a terrible justice from nature. There are consequences for a shortsighted, profit-driven motive. As Teilhard knew, "We can only be saved by becoming one with the universe."[9] Sabbath's call is to stop our ceaseless labor and notice the gifts of creation. To give gratitude is to live differently. Creation is eager and ready to be our companion. She will begin to change our mind and way of being in the world if we walk with her long enough. As I found out, creation can awaken us from a very human-centric life—from amnesia to gratitude.

REVERENCE FOR LIFE

Sabbath time in nature has also taught me reverence. Reverence is respect for and a veneration of something or someone larger than ourselves. As our Sabbath companion, creation calls us to wonder and awe. We are called to set aside our human agenda and go out into a much bigger world than we can even imagine. Our mind, body, and heart can be stunned by starry constellations, tiny salamanders, the endless seething sea with whelks washed up on her sandy flanks.

The French-German organist and theologian Albert Schweitzer became renowned as a nineteenth-century missionary doctor to Africa. Highly gifted and equipped, he determined after his theological studies that he must choose a practical vocation that would allow him to alleviate suffering—not just sit in an ivory tower preaching and postulating about the infinite theological issues of evil, suffering, life, and death. His life, which spanned two world wars, was spent in service in Africa. Schweitzer was deeply affected by the brutality and barbaric evil that gripped the world during these wars, as well as the suffering he encountered in Africa. For Schweitzer, it wasn't just the inhumane crimes of human against human, but the suffering that war visited upon all creation. It became his life vocation to seek out a mission statement that would encompass the breadth of his experiences and his deepest convictions. Eventually he would settle on a theology called "reverence for life." He wrote:

> The great fault of all ethics hitherto has been that they believed themselves to have to deal only with the relations of man to man. In reality, however, the question is what is his attitude to the world and all of life that comes within his reach? A man is ethical only when life, as such, is sacred to him, that of plants and animals as that of his fellow men, and when he devotes himself helpfully to all life that is in need of help.[10]

For Schweitzer, reverence for life calls us back to the Garden of Eden, the place where Sabbath originated. The place of shalom, with roots in Sabbath. A place of wholeness. Of well-being for all.

Since ministry usually kept me buttoned in place, Sabbath Mondays with creation as companion often ended in my backyard. Over time my husband and I began to see our backyard as an extension of our human family, expanding our awareness, evoking reverence. We were terminally interdependent and could not just readily leave its tending to someone else. We became attuned to our backyard birds' rhythms of cheerful song early in the morning. The hummingbird migrations in the fall and their reappearance in the spring. The hawks' predator habits. And when mourning doves' nests were raided by local cats, we were saddened. We noticed the pollinators returning when the lavender started blooming. The cherry tree and the tomatoes all had their own essence to be revealed in season. They had become community. It took time to develop a relationship with the world around us, alive with its own song of creation.

Reverence begins in our backyards. Children must be taught a reverence for life at home. It must be felt and conveyed from the heart place, instilled from a very young age. I believe this reverence is innate in a newborn child, but without nurture it will shrivel. Today children are facing a nature deficit. Continuously plugged in, they live virtual lives through artificial screens. Many will never leave the concrete to face moments of overwhelming infiniteness in nature. And they are suffering from a loss of connection to that which is different from their own anthropological perspective and situation. Without a sense of the "other" in nature, and a return to awe, wonder, and the mystery beyond our small minds, we will not care for nature as part of our tribe. And that would be a huge loss. As Senegalese poet and environmentalist Baba Dioum says, "In the end we will conserve only what we love, we will love only what we understand, and we will understand only what we are taught."[11]

NATURE'S HOSPITALITY

My Sabbath time in creation—on Mondays and during my extended sabbaticals—ushered me into an extravagant hospitality. As Lauren Winner writes, creation's overarching generosity has always been at the root of Sabbath hospitality:

Christians and Jews hold in common one theological basis for hospitality: Creation. Creation is the ultimate expression of God's hospitality to His creatures. In the words of one rabbi, everything God created is "a manifestation of His kindness. [The] world is one big hospitality inn."[12]

I would also experience human hospitality in the years to come from my congregation. Though I didn't often feel such an unconditional sense of "home" in the human world as I did in nature—rife as it was with the complexity of human subjectivity, judgment, and emotion within myself and between others—I would find a soft place to fall in homes of hospitality. Even as something began to shift in my soul, calling me beyond my work in the congregation, this continued to be a saving grace in the midst of it all.

Tending Your Sabbath Soul

1. Share one or two of your favorite spots in nature that conjure up the experience of beauty. Talk about what they mean to you.

2. What about the Celtic understanding of the "Big Book" of creation and the "Little Book" of scripture surprises you? Resonates? Seems familiar?

3. "Shabbat shalom" is a greeting that invokes peaceful relationship with all living beings, a vision that no longer sees creation as utilitarian but as intrinsically valuable. How would this change the world you enter every day if you kept Sabbath with this in mind?

4. Can you share a story or a snapshot of how nature has revealed and extended generous hospitality to you, or when she has been a Sabbath companion for you?

5. Where in your communities do you see a vision of a new interdependent "companioning" with creation? How might shared Sabbath practices in creation inspire and call forth all ages to respond to the crisis of her destruction?

4

SABBATH HOSPITALITY
The Sacrament of Welcoming

We do not find the meaning of life by ourselves
alone—we find it with another.

—THOMAS MERTON, *Love and Living*

MAKING SPACE FOR WELCOME

Facing change is a complex endeavor. Often when we're finally ready to face our life, when we can no longer look away from the need to assess and evaluate our circumstances, we're tired, we're weary, we're ground down. It's easy to dwell on the "cons" side of a pros-and-cons list, but when discerning the way forward both sides deserve deep consideration.

I began to ponder life beyond congregational ministry as I felt my tiredness. There were parts me of that couldn't see any avenue to reviving my soul other than swift and total departure. But then I remembered my people and the generous outpouring of support, kindness, and giving that played a significant role in shaping who I had become over those years. What would I be losing if I stepped away from that loving community embrace? Who would I be if I were no longer the recipient of this sacred hospitality?

In my first years in ministry, I was treading a steep learning curve. I was a young, single, female Mennonite minister, with no mentors for this new calling of being a solo pastor in a congregation. My model for ministry was a large traditional church in rural Ohio, not a small urban congregation. The issues my people struggled with were not the same. Rural issues of farming, small town businesses, and attrition of population were supplanted by undocumented immigrants, nuclear labs, and population growth. The church was no longer the social as well as the spiritual hub of the community. A million and one activities, including soccer on Sundays, vied for the attention of families. I was also struggling not to feel like an imposter as a woman in the pulpit. Nothing in my upbringing had ever groomed me to see myself as a pastoral leader.

Hospitality was integral to my health, I came to find out. It saved my skin many times in those first years. Sunday was not a Sabbath for me since I was technically working. After church services on Sunday I would be so utterly spent that I certainly wasn't up to welcoming people around my table, as I thought a proper pastor should. But my congregation knew what to do. There was no lack of meal invitations from this community of people with whom I had fallen in love. The proffered hospitality allowed me to relax from the fast-paced duties of Sunday mornings and deepen my relationships with my congregants. I felt loved. I belonged. It was something that nourished me well during my early years of ministry.

Come to find out, their hospitality was a charism, a gift that this congregation offered to one another and those who came through our doors. Welcoming the other valued relationship above and beyond stuff and schedules. As we gathered around the table, our human connection evoked at a deep level that which was not achievable through artificial passing pleasantries. Skimming across the surface of our life might require less time and effort, but it leaves us lonelier and more spiritually impoverished. Hospitality can heal.

On the spiritual path, monastics speak of two ways of experiencing the Divine. Apophatic or *via negativa* and kataphatic or *via positiva*. The apophatic tradition is about meeting God by emptying out, facing the void of silence or meditation—it is the place of wilderness or deconstruction of our life. *Via negativa* is about meeting the Holy in that languageless chasm of nothingness—St. John of the Cross identified with "nada" in his dark night of the soul.

Via positiva, on the other hand, is about meeting God by following the path of love in relationship with others. The Psalms evoke the highs and lows of relationship and emotional attachment, wrestling with oneself in relationship to God or another. As spiritual director and teacher Beverly Lanzetta writes:

> Thus if love is the highest form of expression, the seeker finds meaning following the way of love as the spiritual path. For example, bhakti mystics of India and Sufi mystics, such as Rumi, express in their poetry the profound devotion, overwhelming affectivity, and ecstatic love the soul has for God. Espousal prayer, prayers of thanksgiving, gratitude . . . placing God before you as spouse or intimate friend.[1]

Sabbath hospitality is a path of *via positiva*. I experienced this love with my congregation on Sundays, and I experienced this love on my personal Sabbath Mondays, when my weekly retreat sometimes involved an unrushed lunch or a walking date with a friend, or time spent with my spouse and family. Through this love I began to understand hospitality as a sacrament, as an outward sign of an inward grace, as I have often heard it described. At its root, a sacrament is about making something holy. Though I come from a nonsacramental tradition, I know how I feel when I've experienced holiness. It is like the Eastern practice of bowing to another with the ancient Sanskrit word *namaste* on my tongue—holiness is about honoring the animating Divine Spirit within another.

Though I found myself struggling to offer hospitality to others in my early days of ministry, many people graciously embodied this generosity to me. I was often invited into people's homes, where I began to shake loose my stress as they lovingly prepared meals. The evening meal could take hours as we began with appetizers and wine, moving languidly to a colorful savory soup and bread, then on to the main meal. Finally we might move into another space, perhaps before a cozy fire, for dessert with coffee. Sometimes this Sabbath hospitality unfolded in restaurants where strangers offered a welcoming space for congregants and me to experience a shift in our uptight souls and weary bodies. Such Sabbath encounters became precious times of deepening relationships.

One of the places of Sabbath *via positiva* during my ministry was not in someone's home, but it evoked the very same feelings. At the Norbertine Community near Albuquerque, New Mexico, Patty was always there to welcome me when I came to walk the grounds or sit in the chapel. This was not just a job for Patty, but a calling. No doubt hundreds of people came through each week, yet she always remembered my name with such ease and clarity that I never failed to be astonished. Flashing her beautiful smile, she would say my name and speak the words, "I am so glad you are here today! Make yourself at home. Stay as long as you'd like!" Radiating goodwill, each time she'd give a tidbit, a reminder of ways that I was welcome: the open and inclusive worship space; the upcoming Taizé service; the special room set up for daylong visitors, stocked with a microwave, tea, snacks, and a refrigerator. She never failed to mention that even after the doors were locked I was welcome to stay until I was ready to leave. In one fell swoop she issued a deep sense of trust. I felt seen not only as a body but as a soul. It was sacred hospitality. How rare.

Sacred hospitality, offered with an open heart and a sense of timeless welcome, is distinctly different from that which feels obligatory, a rushed affair, with strings attached. As Catholic theologian Henri Nouwen explains:

> Hospitality means primarily the creation of free space where the stranger can enter and become a friend instead of an enemy. Hospitality is not to change people, but to offer them space where change can take place. It is not to bring men and women over to our side, but to offer freedom not disturbed by dividing lines.[2]

We live in a world that is hungry for communities that can offer peace, loving acceptance, and hospitality—things we associate with home, family, tribe. How can we really be ourselves unless and until we are welcomed in and loved for who we *really* are in these places? For many of us, our life is often held together by thin and fragile webs of community and family that sometimes break. We are borne upon the same tides of loneliness, depression, busyness, consumerism, wars, and rumors of wars. We become compassion fatigued. We need each other.

Activist Ingrid Betancourt came to intimately understand the holy power of relationship when she was a captive of the FARC, the quasi-Marxist guerrilla organization of the Revolutionary Armed Forces of Colombia. In a personal memoir, this French-Colombian citizen chronicles her six long years in captivity after a 2002 kidnapping as then-senator, anti-corruption activist, and Green Party Colombian presidential candidate. Secreted away in the far reaches of jungles, she was often shackled behind concentration camp–style barbed wire and walls, kept in solitary confinement, or forced to march for days.

> There were swarms of mosquitoes, acid-red ants, jungle leprosy, microscopic ticks and midges, piranha-infested rivers, anacondas, scorpions, a baking sun and torrential

rains. There was the putrid stench of the *chontos*, or hand-dug latrines. Meager rations of food were more stomach-turning than edible.[3]

The times allowed with other political prisoners of war became sweeter, knowing that the specter of death loomed large over their heads. In those precious moments, she and the other prisoners made space for welcome, sharing laughter, conversation, poetry, literature, and longings for loved ones. It was here that she understood, in the deepest sense, what sacred hospitality and true intimacy meant.

CREATING SABBATH COMMUNITY

As a space in time to be more fully in relationship, delighting in each other, Sabbath can make us more human. As we rest and spend our precious time with loved ones or strangers, without an agenda—something at a premium in today's culture—we are re-created anew. We tend to think of summer vacation as the time to fill up our tanks again with families and friends. But Sabbath keeping is a *weekly* rhythm to remind us that it takes more than visiting once a year for the fruits of relationship to ripen.

For many generations, cities and towns in tandem with Christian churches required communities to observe Sabbath together on Sunday. Many people still remember the "blue laws" that forbade any business establishment to be open on Sunday for buying and selling. It was a whole community effort to slow down and rest from the workaday world. As a child, I remember that the whole town was shut down. We children played games together or read while our parents rested. After a roast beef dinner, which my mom had in the oven while we were at church, the afternoon stretched before us, empty. Blue laws have disappeared and with them much of the church's authority to create a container for communities to keep from engaging in commerce. Without the support of a whole community, or at least one's family, it is much more difficult to withdraw from the culture around us to keep Sabbath. As I contemplated leaving my congregation's leadership post I wondered what would keep me anchored to Sabbath. The practice of community hospitality and breaking bread with others had created a lovely set-apart space with others much as the Sabbath blue laws of another time and place did.

When Reverend Nanette Sawyer was in graduate school, she lived with a Jewish family who celebrated the Sabbath each week beginning with a meal with family and friends—including Nanette—on Friday night. Together they basked in God's presence and the divine gifts of nourishment and community. As Nanette explains in her book *Hospitality—the Sacred Art*, when we invite others to share in at least part of our Sabbath time, we provide an opportunity to express the receptivity, reverence, and generosity to God that defines hospitality. As an added benefit, the influence of others can help us prioritize the commitment:

> [The] practices of Sabbath keeping are strengthened when we do them together. We expect it of each other and welcome each other into the experience. In community we can set aside time to stop working, stop striving, stop achieving, and simply turn our attention toward one another and toward the sacred. In that context, our gifts to each other of food, time, and attention are an extension of God's gifts to us, a reflection of the Life of life. In and through our community experience, we are gathered and bound together, to use the language of Hildegard of Bingen, into the Life of God that nurtures every living creature.[4]

I'm pretty sure that observing Sabbath will not be sustainable, or become rooted in my life, in our lives, unless it is surrounded and practiced by communities that we are embedded in—our family, friends, neighbors, synagogue, mosque, or congregation. And when I'm talking about family, it can be two people. Little by little, carving out space for hospitality with one another can deepen community and intimate bonds of affection. When a community is on board to share hospitality practices with one another, the fruits are multiplied like the loaves and the fishes. Something special can happen.

Benedictine communities are excellent models of hospitality. During the Dark Ages, an ugly moment of our shared human history, Europe was wrenched by violence, disease, and brutal suppression of creativity, art, and religious expression. In this dearth of human and divine flowering, the Benedictine movement took root. The purpose of Benedictine communities was not necessarily ministering outside the monasteries initially; it was about living together by the Rule. But due to the gravity of the times and what was needed, inevitably their ministry grew to include those who came to their doors. Sick, elderly, poor, pilgrims, guests. All were seen as Christ coming in disguise, and all were treated with the utmost respect and care. In a time of political chaos and increasing meanness and violence, the Benedictines offered a place of comfort, welcome, and peace.

To this day, welcoming the stranger is core to how Benedictine communities operate worldwide. When I lived within a Benedictine community for a brief time, I was overwhelmed by what the community called "conviviality." It was a constant and welcome break from working and living alone. Every Friday night, a meal would be prepared by the dining hall or one of the scholars in residence, and my colleagues and I would all converge around spirits and hearty food for convivial times.

The meals and proffered food and drink for events where people gathered—whether after liturgy, work, or celebration—"greased the wheels" for relationship. I'm certain that it deepened friendships.

Benedict's approach was about human development, according to Joan Chittister, a Benedictine sister, as quoted in her biography:

> It is in the "theology of the community," writes Chittister, where Benedictine spirituality most departs "from the traditional norms of religious life. . . . Of all the places where the Rule of Benedict shows us the real depth of the spiritual life, it is surely in its theology of community. 'The most valiant kind of monk,' Benedict writes from a culture of hermits, is not the solitary or the pseudo-ascetic or the wandering beggar but 'the cenobite' (RB1:12), the one who has learned to live with others in community."[5]

Along with practicing receptivity and reverence to God, sharing Sabbath time in community allows us to benefit from the gifts of reciprocity. By *gifts of reciprocity* I do not necessarily mean the material tit-for-tat that Jesus warns us about in Luke 14:12—"When you give a luncheon or dinner, do not invite your friends, your brothers or sisters, your relatives, or your rich neighbors; if you do, they may invite you back, and so you would be repaid"—but the blessings that come from generosity of spirit with those unlike yourself.

Jean Vanier's life work was about creating community among the least of these, people who are differently abled, physically and mentally. His L'Arche communities for people with developmental disabilities and their helpers are places of hospitality and islands of harmony. Henri Nouwen, the author and Catholic theologian, spent much of his later years living among these "little ones" who, despite how they are viewed on the outside, are filled with an infectious joy, humor, and love. For them, every day is a day to delight in relationship. Vanier tells a story about this delight in an interview:

> I was sitting and there was a man who was a bit glum, like a lot of people, a bit glum. And there was a knock on the door. And before I could say "Come in," Jean Claude walked in, and Jean Claude technically would be Down syndrome. And Jean Claude shook my hand and laughed, and shook the hand of the other fellow and laughed, and went out laughing. And the man that had been in my office looked at me and said, "Isn't it sad, children like that?" What was sad was that he was totally blind. He didn't see that Jean Claude was happy.[6]

Without a future of selling stocks, holding a title, or marrying and creating a family, the L'Arche members find their community in the shared spiritual and daily care practices with one another. People like Nouwen, who come to volunteer, fleeing the vicissitudes of their busy and often lonely work lives, are warmly welcomed and loved back to life. Everyone in the household participates in giving and receiving, sharing in the spiritual plenitude of a unique community. For Nouwen, it was nourishing and restorative. As he fed, bathed, prayed, and spent time with residents, without needing to defend who he was or what he was, he experienced an unconditional love. A powerful experience for anyone. The great circle of relationship—giving and receiving—healed his spirit more than once. It brought him home to peace as he deepened his relationships with other human beings at the heart level. It was a place of true intimacy, which he defines as "the mutuality of our confession of our total self to each other."[7]

TABLE FELLOWSHIP

So much of the hospitality I was gifted as minister flourished around a table. Table fellowship is at the root of most hospitality. It is one of those sacred thresholds for reclaiming what it means to be human with one another. Sabbath space set aside to honor the coming of another and spend time in relationship over food is a place of intimacy. Jesus spent much time in table fellowship. It was a way to honor human interaction of all kinds—across cultural, religious, economic, and gender division. It was in table fellowship that he lifted up the woman who came to anoint him, to the disgust of the men gathered. It was around a table that he called Zacchaeus, the hated tax collector, to follow him. It was around a table that he spent time with every manner of hypocrite, deceiver, liar, and lover. Table fellowship can be a place we take off our masks.

One summer sabbatical my husband and I visited my mother-in-law's home in Atlanta, Georgia. My husband's people are from the Deep South. The rich legacy of southern storytellers, authors, and good preachers is well known. Tapestries of words and vivid, colorful imaginations seem to be bred into the bones of southerners. Or perhaps it is in the water. It is about slowing down long enough to have a decent conversation and hear a good story over a meal. Even if it means civil discourse on dangerous ground, such as politics or religion.

I glimpsed an era gone by as I helped Peggy, my mother-in-law, set the table. Every cupboard was jammed full of crystal glassware and china with patterns for every occasion. Once upon a time, southern hospitality was a ritual that was correct as clockwork. Bringing out the silver tea set with dainty cookies, cheeses, cold cuts, and carefully decorated two-tiered coconut and German chocolate cakes was an art form—along with the conversation that it inspired around the table.

Eventually Peggy invited me to open the cupboards above the refrigerator. I hadn't noticed these large doors before. Inside were silver candlesticks and candy dishes, platters and chalices. The silver shone in that rich glossy way that it does when polished. I marveled at the fact that it still held its shine and wasn't tarnished. Silver guestware was definitely not something in the homes of my generation. Cabinet after cabinet that I opened was packed with multitudes of "sets"—Thanksgiving, Easter, birthday, Christmas.

I could only begin to imagine the life of table fellowship that my now diminutive eighty-year-old mother-in-law had hosted in her life. Now she couldn't even give away these gobs of crystal glasses, sets of flatware, silver, and china for all occasions. My generation and those that came after had lost the body memory, the craft, but most of all the time, for this most basic but practical and exquisite domestic art—welcoming others into one's home with your best, whatever that may be.

Table fellowship on Sabbath is rooted in an unshakeable fidelity to that which is local, abiding in present time. Our dining room tables—as we collect around them each week—become a shared feast of relief from the lonely struggle of eking out a little bit of time, energy, or money. As we throw open the doors, cease working, and come to the table, this weekly space in time is freed up and becomes a hearth of gladness and shared anticipation.

EXTENDING HOSPITALITY TO OURSELVES

My years of ministry were busy and fruitful times. I learned to respond, respond, respond, reaching out constantly. But it was much harder to extend hospitality to myself.

I had bought into the busyness trap, a term coined by Tim Kreider, author of *We Learn Nothing*. This trap is about running ourselves ragged, booking every waking moment with so many activities that we are left breathless—but not so breathless we can't crow about our productivity. He writes:

> If you live in America in the twenty-first century you've probably had to listen to a lot of people tell you how busy they are. It's become the default response when you ask anyone how they're doing: "Busy!" "*So* busy." "*Crazy* busy!" It's pretty obviously a boast disguised as a complaint.[8]

Kreider suspects our busyness has become a middle-class disease to disguise our ambition, our anxiety, our fear of true intimacy, beginning with ourselves. Could our frantic days really just be, as Kreider says, a "hedge against emptiness," camouflage for our hidden dread that if we faced our addiction to busyness we'd have to confront our loneliness or the fact that our life is trivial, meaningless?[9]

Turns out, one of the lasting lessons from my time with my congregation was the importance of offering hospitality to myself. Even as I grappled with my own "perfect pastor" image of being a capable host, I came to realize that unless I was rested myself, offering hospitality would only call up resentment and irritation. As Jean Vanier writes, "If the heart is not peaceful, it cannot welcome."[10]

Whether our busyness is a form of escape or a drive to be indispensable to those we love and serve, this manic ambition often leaves us sapped of creative energy and strength for our work. It leaves us unavailable in body and spirit to those we love, and unable to recognize our true selves. Sabbath keeping counters this mania, replacing our hollow hyperactivity with precious hospitable space for rest and meaning making. As Kreider concludes:

Idleness is not just a vacation, an indulgence or a vice; it is as indispensable to the brain as vitamin D is to the body, and deprived of it we suffer a mental affliction as disfiguring as rickets. The space and quiet that idleness provides is a necessary condition for standing back from life and seeing it whole.[11]

As Benedictine monk Daniel Homan and author Lonni Collins Pratt point out in their book *Radical Hospitality: Benedict's Way of Love*, perhaps we are the strangers in need of sacred hospitality:

There is a kind of gentle hospitality with the self that most of us fail to practice. You know that moment you look in the mirror and see a stranger staring out those eyes? We don't accept the stranger within. We dread the regions of ourselves we don't understand.[12]

SABBATH COMMUNION FOR BODY AND SOUL

In her article "Joy Unspeakable in an Unspeakably Joyless World," author and ethics professor Barbara Holmes writes that "materialism and consumerism are poor substitutes for the refreshment of spiritual joy."[13] In our world, much of the way we've been taught to relate to ourselves and others is through the acquisition of stuff, buying time and attention for ourselves and others. When we create time for our own sacred hospitality, something akin to mystery can be unleashed by the simple act of welcoming our own body.

Our bodies are the gateway to our souls. Indeed, they are indivisible from our souls. As Episcopal priest and theologian Barbara Brown Taylor explains, mostly we have been told of a dualistic split between body and spirit:

Here we sit, with our souls tucked away in this marvelous luggage, mostly insensible to the ways in which
every spiritual practice begins with the body. Our bodies have shaped our views of the world, just as our world
has shaped our views of our bodies.[14]

In her beautiful classic on body theology, *An Altar in the World:
A Geography of Faith,* Taylor tackles all our misshapen ideas about
sex that have come to us, particularly in our Judeo-Christian
tradition. She makes the point that our bodies are what ultimately connect us to other people. Wearing skin is not a solitary practice but a communal one. It is what we most have in
common. Despite a healthy, earthy theology in Genesis—that of
bodies formed out of the good soil—Christianity seems to have
absorbed the cultural, dualistic split early on. Perhaps as far back
as the Greeks and the early Gnostic Christians, they shunned the
world in order to achieve spiritual enlightenment or oneness with
God through intellectual knowledge. But first-century incarna-
tional Christianity was—and still is—not this.

In her chapter "The Practice of Wearing Skin," Taylor writes:

We would rather lock up our bodies than listen to
what they have to say. Where Christians are concerned,
this leaves us in the peculiar position of being followers of the Word Made Flesh who neglect our own
flesh—or worse—who treat our bodies with shame
and scorn.[15]

The Jewish Jesus welcomed suffering bodies and souls on the Sabbath. There was a woman whose body, over eighteen long years,
had become stooped, her osteoporotic spine deformed, "crippled
by a spirit," the storyteller said. Jesus saw her on the Sabbath.
Compassion overcame him. "Woman, you are set free from your

infirmity," he proclaimed, as his hands, gentle with kindness, rested on her body. I can imagine her breath catching as she felt her spine straighten. She stood up, stunned and ecstatic. But the religious leaders were not going to let this go easy. Bypassing Jesus, they went for the jugular of the people. Lips snarling, they reminded the worshippers that there were six days to be healed. *Go away and come back on one of those days if you have a problem. How dare the Sabbath be used for healing. Holy days are made for rest.* But Jesus was no shrinking violet. He chastised the leaders, thoroughly humiliating them. He sarcastically pointed out that they took care of their animals on this day, so why shouldn't a daughter of Abraham and Sarah, bound up for so long in her body, also be freed? The people loved it.[16]

There is a neighborhood lunch joint in Atlanta called Souper Jenny. Visiting one day, I was taken aback by this unapologetically female-owned and -operated eating establishment. Everywhere I turned, there was joyful curvy artwork celebrating food and health. My favorite was a huge portrait of a bowl with the words above it, *Life itself is a proper binge!* The bathroom was dedicated to pithy quotes. As I sat on the throne, I read the posted motto on the wall in front of me:

Thoughts on Whole Living

Your body is a powerful healer. Eat to nourish it. Take control of your time. Aim to be strong and flexible and balanced. Exercise for vitality, not vanity. Sleep is sacred, nurture it with a soothing, restful space. Learn to embrace the cold, it helps you appreciate the warmth. Eating better doesn't take more time, just better choices. Rediscover sex as a life-giving energy. Stress plays a key role in your life, don't let it rule you. Moving forward starts with letting go.

I came to know through my own journey that until bodies are offered hospitality in their fullness and wholeness in our faith communities, especially on the Sabbath, we will be less than a people of the Living One. If we don't talk about the beautiful, fierce power of our bodies, which resides together with our souls, then we will do both a disservice.

The hungers gnawing at the body and soul are legion. We walk through our lives trying to ignore or sublimate them. Though we may be familiar with the idea of an excessive and obsessive focus on sex, we are less aware of something just as tragic—sexual anorexia. This is an unhealthy constriction and restriction of the part of ourselves that is gendered and fleshy. We come to believe that a part of ourselves is not welcomed or acceptable. As a result, our body and soul become estranged from each other. That alienation then manifests in our relationships with others. Yet our sexuality is indivisible from our soul. For starters, I am talking about a broader definition of sex than purely the act of coitus. I am talking about all the ways we are shaped and formed as gendered beings, not just in our body parts but in our emotional bodies.

In our society and communities, others respond to the configuration of body. It affects how we feel about ourselves, how we move about in the world, how we perceive that others feel about us, how others treat us, and how, then, we treat our own bodies. Because these external messages are so powerful, it is critical that our religious culture model true hospitality to our bodies— whether differently abled, mentally ill, married, single, straight, or other gendered. Replacing pious religiosity, shunning, and a deep-seated fear with true human intimacy will heal our wounds. Here our deepest feelings, fears, longings, hopes, and passions are welcomed. Sabbath can be a home for our bodies and souls to experience communion and welcome. A place to deepen intimacy with not only others, but with the creation and ourselves.

Imam Jamal Rahman tells a story about a Muslim Sufi elder of a village in Bangladesh. He told Rahman once that the "reason God gave us a human body is that the body makes us aware of what needs our attention and love on the spiritual plane. By greeting our physical sensations with awareness and compassion, we move closer to the divine Heart."[17]

I had strayed far from the requirements of my flesh, and Sabbath keeping was a way to return, an offering of hospitality to my body. Here, in my own temple of atoms and flesh, bone, muscle, and sinew, Sabbath time offered a space to renew and reenergize my body. The Sabbath space waited patiently for me, week after week, to step outside my daily routine and enjoy life more. But I had to be willing to seize this opportunity to offer hospitality to my body.

Rabbi Abraham Joshua Heschel is unabashed in his teachings on Jewish Sabbath as a time for enjoying our bodies for pleasure. It is a time for sexual delight with one's beloved. Hebraic culture, which could've been seen as downright randy in the earliest stages of the tribes of Israel becoming God's people, surely celebrated sexuality in its holy books.

In the biblical story of Song of Songs, eroticism is readily intertwined with soul. On a superficial level, the Song of Songs is a love poem between a woman and a man. On a deeper, spiritual level, scriptural interpreters in the Jewish tradition read the Song as an expression of God's love for Israel, and in the Christian tradition as Christ's love for his beloved church. Certainly, as in all cultures, there was an emphasis on the virility of youth. Still, the awaited joyful coupling of the lovers is celebrated. Their encounters are deliciously recalled, their longing is legend. These lovers may be from another time, but we know their passion in our own bones—even if it is from a bygone era of youthfulness.

My lover is to me a sachet of myrrh
Resting between my breasts.
My lover is to me a cluster of henna blossoms
From the vineyards of En Gedi.
How beautiful you are, my darling!
Oh, how beautiful!
Your eyes are doves.
How handsome you are, my beloved!
Oh, how charming!
And our bed is verdant.
The beams of our house are cedars;
Our rafters are firs.
—Song of Songs 1:13–17

C. S. Lewis writes about an erotic God who delights in pleasure in *The Weight of Glory*. This pleasure encompasses more than just good sex. In this sermon Lewis cites another of his books, *The Screwtape Letters,* where an elder demon, Screwtape, is mentoring the younger Wormwood on the best ways to trip up humans. Screwtape cautions the little devil-in-training never to forget "that when we are dealing with any pleasure in its healthy and normal and satisfying form, we are, in a sense, on the Enemy's ground."[18]

Pleasure is God's invention and the world is full of God's pleasures, despite the ways they have been twisted and abused.

By keeping Sabbath, I was learning what hospitality to my body looked like. As I experienced the pleasures of being a body each week—not just an intellect or a spirit dancing about this earthly plane—I found new, unexplored inner landscapes begin to beckon me. It was a renaissance of energy. I was a dancing body. I was a painting body. I was a singing body. A writing body. A beekeeping body. Unexpectedly, I wondered if it was time to leave my ministry post. Perhaps a new form of work awaited me? I hungered for a renewed sense of joy in more areas of my life, unbridled by the need to be responsive to so much and so many. But who would I be without the community that extended so much welcome to me and a deep sense of home?

Tending Your Sabbath Soul

1. Jean Vanier said that "if the heart is not peaceful, it cannot welcome." What brings your heart peace? How much time do you spend in that space or place?

2. An example of Sabbath hospitality is the Rule of Benedict, which became a balm for human communities suffering during a very dark age. Where do you see such hospitality offering healing in today's world?

3. Describe the busyness trap in your life.

4. What would it mean to carve out a weekly Sabbath table fellowship space for family and community? How might it change your relationships?

5. Reflect on Sabbath as a space of healing. How have you experienced healing in your body and soul as you kept Sabbath? Or not? What would it take to create such a space of Sabbath hospitality for healing to happen?

6. What have you been taught about pleasure? Consider how Sabbath keeping might help you enjoy and welcome your body and soul and connect to another's.

5

CULTIVATING JOY

The Sabbath Path of Creativity, Contemplation, and Play

Joy is the most infallible sign of the presence of God.
—LÉON BLOY, letter to Jacques Maritain

AWAKENING TO CREATIVITY

My appetite and restlessness for a more joyful way of living, a different way of being, was undeniable. Parts of myself that had lain dormant and hungry were now awakened, thanks to Sabbath keeping practices. Yet when I envisioned my life outside of ministry, it was as if I had jumped off a cliff, swum far out into the ocean with no horizon in sight. Who would I be? How would I function without my identity as a pastor? It was uncomfortable and scary. I was terrified of the undertow. I sorted through a wilderness of anxieties. *How would I be useful to the world if I left my ministry? How would I be of service?* But I could no longer shake off the nagging feeling that I needed to change direction.

Fortunately, Sabbath keeping gave me both the tools to begin the discernment of a new direction in my life and the courage to finally move with this new current. One of the fruits of Sabbath during that discernment time was a reawakening of creativity. The flourishing of creativity, whether through singing, writing, beekeeping, or just ambling along the river with my own thoughts, allowed me to ponder the change happening in the depths of my being. This awakening gave me the courage to finally make a decision. As writer Sue Monk Kidd so aptly puts it, "We will have a true and blissful marriage to life only to the extent that we are aware."[1]

Creativity wakes us up. It is the elixir that can sustain and nourish a joyful life, bubbling up to the surface. For this sweetness to rise up within us, we need both space and time. The fallow time of Sabbath is not just a stern command. It also allows our soul to let its hair down, so to speak. In my journal, halfway through my ministry, I wrote, "I have repressed my feminine side, unbeknownst to me . . . the spiritual gestation, labor, and birth of a large part of my soul. The sorrow overwhelms me these days. I have repressed her for too long. She has become incorrigible within me, that soul child. She has waited too long for my attention. 'Give me time!' she demands." That feminine side was my creative, receptive muse, longing for the God of Sabbath.

For children, idle time is necessary to stimulate the imagination and provide space to joyfully create unhindered. It is no different for adults. It seems that some of the best human inventions have come from daydreaming and reflection time. I know how it opens up reservoirs of creativity for me when I have time on my hands. Sometimes it's a trickle, sometimes it becomes a flood. It all depends on how much time is thrown open.

This kind of time is not *chronos* time, based upon a wristwatch. It is *kairos* time, God's time. *Kairos,* a Greek word, literally means an opportune moment in time. It can signal time pregnant with divine potential. It is a graced moment, beyond our control. We have the choice to make room for *kairos* time, but we cannot force its hand. When *kairos* breaks into the human condition, it is like the dawn of the morning sun. We can participate only in the present moment. *Kairos* time is "time that is beyond time, time in which we become what we are called on to be and when we feel our creativity as though we are co-creators with God," writes religion and mythology scholar Joseph Campbell.[2]

The kind of creativity generated during *kairos* time is not so much about a need to become an accomplished artist, a new Bob Dylan or Picasso of our generation, as it is about being fully awake and truly alive, as spiritual teacher and minister Jane Vennard writes in her book by the same name.[3] She talks about the four steps of the creative process first proposed in 1926 by English social psychologist Graham Wallas in his book *The Art of Thought*. These include:

1. Preparation
2. Incubation
3. Illumination
4. Implementation

While all four stages can take place during Sabbath time, it is the second stage, incubation, that is the generative wonder. It requires time. Space. As Vennard explains:

> We need to let go of trying to figure everything out, think everything through to completion. The image I use for this incubation stage is a game of pick-up sticks, when we toss the sticks into the air and see what pattern is formed in their landing. Up goes all that preparation so that a new idea can be born, one we most likely could not have come to with our rational minds.[4]

She says resting does not guarantee that we'll be gifted amazing new insights, "but without letting go and resting, we are likely to simply rehash old ideas, focus on what is already before us, rearrange the known facts, and never come up with anything new."[5] Albert Einstein is famous for saying that the same mind-set that created a problem cannot solve it.

For me, Sabbath Monday was adult playtime, a tantalizing taste of what could happen if the sap of creativity were allowed to rise even more than one day a week. Some days I would make a fire, pull out my table with my watercolors, and become lost in delight for hours at a time. Or I would put on music and dance in my living room. Suddenly the morning would be gone. New avenues of exploring a topic or an idea would emerge. Creative sparks flew. Sometimes the painting under my brush gave me an inkling of the midwifing process unfolding within. But how could this live side by side with the demanding schedule of my job?

Mary Oliver examines the creative life in her book *Upstream*. She talks about the importance of concentration, hard to find in today's highly distracted world, and the need for giving oneself to the work at hand. If the creative, restless spirit is rising in you, you will ever be regretful if you don't make time for it.[6] I knew I had a choice. I felt a surge, tugging me in a new direction at fifty years old. If I ignored the call once again, the last part of my life would be charted away from unknown joys I had yet to explore. If I said yes, I would certainly face the chaos and uncertainty that change imposes upon one's life when awakened to creativity. But I would also drink from a deeper well of joy. At least that was the hope. As Oliver explains, the poet Walt Whitman unabashedly called our attention to "a better, richer life . . . available to us, and with all his force he advocated it both for the good of each individual soul and for the good of the universe."[7]

The world is always going to come around us, calling us forth to its dizzying bedazzlement. That's the nature of earth's material manifestation. But if the self continues to shut down and distract the creative muse of our own soul, as Mary Oliver well knows, being unrequited can take a toll on our spirit. She writes:

> The world sheds, in the energetic way of an open and communal place, its many greetings, as a world should. What quarrel can there be with that? But that the self can interrupt the self—and does—is a darker and more curious matter.[8]

The fact that we allow ourselves to be endlessly distracted and interrupted makes me wonder what happens to the collective soul of our religious and educational institutions, a nation that has no time for creativity, no space to reflect on our life together. Does it create a loss of consciousness? Is that the darkness that Oliver is referring to? When we become a nation living only at a shallow level, as reflected in our political sphere, lobbing the same bombs of uncreative responses toward one another?

Living into a new imagination, a new way of being together as humankind, needs our fullest creative genius. It requires loyalty of time and focused energy. We must consecrate, make holy, our time and refuse distractions whether it be the telephone, the dental appointment that needs to be made, the dishes and the laundry waiting. Without the creative process—whether in art, science, education, or religion—an imaginative reflection and response will wither. It is what sets us apart from automatons and machines. It is what makes us a part of the unfolding creation—ancient, wise, and evolving. Unexpected things can bloom and sometimes that which is magnificently extraordinary can surprise us. Our personal lives and institutions will be richer if we create containers of safety and space for human creativity to blossom. One of those containers is the deep silence of solitude.

ALTARS OF SABBATH SOLITUDE

Sabbath practice during my ministry began to strip away things from my life. It was taking me to the basics. At my core, I began to touch the beating heart of the monastic contemplative. It was the womb of the Beloved. The place where I was unconditionally received, totally and completely. I realized that I wanted more of this fertile solitude.

In her book *The Call of Solitude*, psychoanalyst Ester Buchholz writes:

> Solitude is required for the unconscious to process and unravel problems. Others inspire us, information feeds us, practice improves our performance, but we need quiet time to figure things out, to emerge with new discoveries, to unearth original answers.[9]

The uncomfortable truth was that somewhere along the journey, the very public and ceaseless ebb and flow of congregational ministry had given me professional security, but was washing me farther and farther away from my own soul. Times of Sabbath solitude created a longing to swim out into that vast sea of unknown potential rather than be safe in the harbor of what I knew. In my growing discontent, I knew it was time to leave my post in the congregation. It was a painful realization. It took years to finally let go. I loved my community. But by the time I released my hold, it was clear that inside my soul I ached for more solitude in my life. After years of agonizing over this decision, I was finally ready to take the plunge. I wrapped up my ministry and struck out into uncharted waters.

Eighteen months after I took the leap out of full-time ministry, the nation was wracked by a brutal political season. Fortunately, one of the gifts of my decision to leave ministry to follow my heart was a scholar-in-residence fellowship. On the eve of one of the most hostile, rude, and increasingly uncivilized elections in remembered history, my soul felt bruised. The election only emphasized the divided times we were living in—the vast economic and social inequities, the growing chasm of ecological ills. I needed to lean into my faith, a place of grounding for me. So I sat for Vespers with the Benedictine brothers of St. John's in Collegeville, Minnesota, where I resided. I waited in the solitude of that dark night with those monks. Soon the songs and Psalms of wretchedness and refuge rose and fell around me. As if in a tidal pool, I suddenly had a sense of floating in a vast eternal sea. Perhaps I had finally plunged into the depths of the sea that I had been longing for earlier in my discernment. I looked around at the sturdy community of brothers that would continue unabated, no matter the outcome of the election. These monks had been here continuously for hundreds of years, building a life sustained by contemplation. They would remain, come what may. They passed along the Benedictine rule of wise living and stewardship for the commonwealth. It almost seemed to be in their spiritual genetics. Whatever seethed around them, their lives would remain anchored in this contemplative rhythm. Community, work, prayer. A peaceful bird settled in me that evening, a sure sense that some things were unchanging. Immutable. In a way similar to the brothers, I knew I needed to yoke myself to a life more deeply infused with the solitude of prayer from this night going forth. Paula Huston, writer and oblate of the Camaldolese Benedictine Monastics of Big Sur, names the necessity of prayer:

> Without prayer, we are in danger of perishing of spiritual thirst, no matter how firmly we hold our beliefs. How do we recover our connection with prayer? We are to see the biblical heart, that "organ of prayer," within us . . . designed to be in continual contact with God.

When we finally come upon it, we discover something truly amazing: our heart, like an intricate clock set into motion at baptism, is already praying on its own. However, unless we reduce the clamor around us and quiet down ourselves, it is nearly impossible to hear it.[10]

The monks take the concept of a whole day of Sabbath—ceasing our labor and business as usual—and break it down into bite-sized morsels, which I experienced with the monks. An ancient fixed prayer, it is required seven times daily for some monastics. Every ordinary day of work has a piece of Sabbath in it. You don't need to enter an order or be cloistered to reduce the noise in your life, only listen to the drumming of your own Sabbath rhythm, with others or alone. The late editor and writer Phyllis Tickle, a favorite spiritual teacher whom I had the distinct privilege of interviewing once, practiced these monastic Divine Hours throughout the day. Every three hours, every single day, her wristwatch would go off, sending her to a quiet place to pray or read the Psalms aloud. Phyllis described her practice in this way:

> Discipline is growing a muscle. And this is discipline. It's the growing of the spiritual muscle. It's the discipline that allows you even to check out, sometimes, when you're in the middle of a meeting, for instance, or in the middle of a high-pressure conversation and that watch beeps.[11]

For her it was less about being a devout Christian or Episcopalian, and more about being simply human, offering herself to God in a constant and ceaseless prayer—a posture inviting inquiry, curiosity, and joy.

A life with Sabbath solitude built in is simply an examined life, day by day, portable in every aspect of our existence.

Nothing fancier than that. As we acknowledge and sit at the altars of silence and solitude regularly, our life becomes attuned to what really matters in all aspects of living. Finding our altars of solitude can be as simple as taking a moment from the computer to go for a walk, or sitting at a stoplight in traffic and allowing the consolations and desolations of the day to rise up and be released as a prayer and a sorrow or joy. In *One Minute Wisdom* Jesuit Anthony de Mello relates the following conversation:

> Said the Master to the businessman: "As the fish perishes on dry land, so you perish when you get entangled in the world. The fish must return to the water—you must return to solitude."
>
> The businessman was aghast. "Must I give up my business and go into the monastery?"
>
> "No, no. Hold onto your business and go into your heart."[12]

Once the taproot of solitude deepened within myself, I became more mindful. I found it easier to know when I became saturated, my soul craving silence. A key indicator was a rising tide of anxiety or overwhelm, often followed by a short temper or tears with those closest to me. When this happened, I stopped to examine my life. *When was the last time I set aside dedicated time or took a true Sabbath to listen?* Struggling with severe anxiety as a young woman, I found it was this mindfulness that allowed me to sustain my ministry without being eaten alive from the inside.

This life of regular silence or solitude is also called a contemplative life. It is not a means to an end. I see the contemplative path as a way to expand my imagination regularly. It invites me to wholehearted living and encourages a willingness to explore a fuller way of being with all the joy, beauty, and suffering life offers. Some of the most joyful persons I know are not wealthy, clever, accomplished, or renowned. A friend of mine, an organic farmer who cherishes the land he tills and serves, recovered from a serious heroin addiction after years on the horse jockey circuit. The sport had become dehumanizing and brutal. He left that world "out there" and all its demands, returning to the little plot of family land awaiting him. There, he connected with the earth and its quieter, more subtle rhythms. In other words, a contemplative life. As he slowed down to examine his life, he became attuned to his thought patterns and feelings. No longer a slave to his thoughts and actions, he could make life-affirming choices. He became strong enough to let go of his addiction. He calls this examined life "the inner witness." It saved his life. He is one of the most joyful persons I know, with a great reverence for all matter.

As Thomas Merton explains:

> Contemplation . . . is spiritual wonder. It is spontaneous awe at the sacredness of life, of being. . . . It is a vivid realization of the fact that life and being in us proceed from an invisible, transcendent, and infinitely abundant source. Contemplation is, above all, awareness of the reality of that source. It *knows* the Source, obscurely, inexplicably, but with a certitude that goes both beyond reason and beyond simple faith.[13]

Contemplation born out of Sabbath time eventually gave me the inner resources and capacity to look at all of my life with a more clear-eyed, honest gaze. It allowed me to choose not to bypass self-growth and wisdom either in my professional life or, eventually, my personal life for the riches they offered. It is what gave me the ability to make the decision, finally, to leave everyone and everything that defined me in the ministry. What seemed like professional suicide became a door to personal and spiritual growth. It was the opening to more play.

SABBATH PLAY

Creatures naturally play. Their nature is to "be" as they were created. They do not strive to acquire more than they need. Or be anything other than their intended nature. There is a heartwarming story of creaturely play in the work of Ellen Meloy, one of the great Western ecological writers of our time. In her last book, *Eating Stone: Imagination and the Loss of the Wild,* she retells a story of her time with the great bighorn sheep of the West. She chronicles their struggle to survive on the razor's edge of "civilization." From her endless hours, days, and weeks spent outdoors watching the sheep—ewes, lamb, and rams—she captures the spirit of play in this largely social but remote and isolated herd of wild creatures:

> They rise from their day beds and break into random frolics. Even the heavy-bellied older ewes move about with great animation. It is almost as if the whole band has been eating funny plants.
>
> Instigated mostly by the yearlings, the sheep fill their stone world with feisty play. One butts a companion off a shrub and is then butted off the shrub by another sheep. Soon everyone is butting everyone else off their shrubs. A gang of yearlings begins to butt everything in sight. They butt rocks, yucca plants, a prickly pear cactus, the air, one another. Two yearling rams put themselves in reverse, then charge each other with a loud clonk of horns.
>
> A sleek young ewe with a small face and a dark cape jumps straight up in the air like a piece of toast. Toast pops spread throughout the band like a chain reaction. There are chases and leaps and races along knife-edged ledges above sixty-foot drops.

A chasm of sandstone becomes a game. Several sheep line up and leap across it. . . . The next sheep rushes down one wall and straight up the other.

The last sheep tries the same maneuver but doesn't make the second jump. It leaps upward, misses the wall's lip, and in a split-second turns its body in a complete about-face, falls and rushes back up the first wall. Ricocheting sheep.[14]

Whether human or creaturely, play is one of the ways we communicate joy and delight. Vitamins that the soul needs in order to be nourished and rejuvenated are found in healthy play. Sabbath carves out time for play, something children naturally do. As masterful players, they revel in their unabashed need for it. As William Wordsworth said, children come from God, "trailing clouds of glory."[15] Heaven's joy is expressed in their playful delight. It is found in their fresh-faced and rapt attention to the wonders of the earth. We see joy in their warm affections and desire to love and be loved. Jesus of the New Testament held up children as beacons of the Kingdom of Heaven—the transformation of our whole beings, inside and out. Although his disciples tried to stem the flow of children drawn to him, Jesus picked them up, sat with them, and loved them.

What keeps us from ceasing work for play? I had become driven by my work. A little too much ego was wrapped up in it. Perhaps somewhere deep inside, I knew that if I took time for Sabbath play with others, something would be released in me that could be at once exciting, confusing, and anxiety producing. It's true. Play is about a return to our inner child, which can be awkward at first. But the exhilaration that play can unearth also leads to new levels of joy. A turning point for me was when dancer, storyteller, player, and community gatherer Cynthia Winton Henry invited me to attend a weeklong Interplay retreat near Santa Fe.[16]

I couldn't quite fathom leaving my work for that long. But somewhere in my exhausted soul I heard, *Go*. That week we danced and made meaning through laughter, play, and shared stories. It was one of the creative intersections where I strengthened my resolve to explore new avenues in my life, beyond how I had come to define myself. At the retreat, new things about myself showed up in that circle of playmates. I gathered the courage to step outside my comfort zone where I was no longer the expert. I became the learner, alongside others.

Dr. Stuart Brown, head of the National Institute for Play and author of *Play*, explains why we play:

> Play is something done for its own sake. It's voluntary, it's pleasurable, it offers a sense of engagement, it takes you out of time. And the act itself is more important than the outcome.[17]

Then as now, our culture forces us to be time starved and play deprived. The rules of living in most Western cultures call for less play, exploration, and adventure in favor of a stern adult-style schedule. As writer Mary Oliver puts it, "With growth into adulthood, responsibilities claimed me, so many heavy coats. I didn't choose them, I don't fault them, but it took time to reject them."[18] We are fed the singular lie that we must work endlessly for a better life. Our culture doesn't promote a paradigm to reduce our materialistic appetites so we can work less and play more, and as a result it doesn't take long for joy to be socialized out of a child. We are taught early to advance to the top of the ladder, which is part of the young seeker's journey and often necessary for growth. But eventually we awaken, as I did, only to find that the multitudes of delights that a child knows are forgotten. It is important to notice when and how we begin to move away from our own soul's play and joy. As Dr. Brown explains:

What you begin to see when there's major play deprivation in an otherwise competent adult is that they're not much fun to be around. You begin to see that the perseverance and joy in work is lessened and that life is much more laborious.[19]

Holy merriment is not something we usually associate with God, but play and laughter surely are aspects of the nature of God. Play and good humor can completely change our internal landscape when life has squeezed joy out of us. As naturalist and poet Diane Ackerman describes:

Deep play allows one to feel quintessentially alive, heartbeat by heartbeat, in the eternal present. The here and now becomes a pop-up storybook, full of surprises, in which everything looms. It returns us to the openness of childhood.[20]

There is a story of a child who tries to pay heed to the voice of play:

At a metro station in Washington, D.C., a man started to play the violin. It was a cold January morning. He played six Bach pieces for about forty-five minutes. During that rush hour it was calculated that thousands of people went through the station.

After three minutes, a middle-aged man stopped for a few seconds and then hurried on. A minute later, the violinist received his first dollar tip—tossed in the box by a woman without slowing her stride. A few minutes later, someone leaned against the wall to listen, but after looking at his watch, began to walk quickly on his way.

The one who paid the most attention was a three-year-old boy. His mother hurried him along but the child stopped in front of the violinist. Reluctantly the boy was dragged away, looking back all the time.

During the forty-five minutes that the musician played, only five people stopped and stayed for a while. He collected thirty-two dollars. When he finished playing and silence took over, no one applauded him or showed any sign of recognition.

The violinist was Joshua Bell, one of the world's finest musicians. He had played some of the most intricate pieces ever written, with a violin worth 3.5 million dollars.[21]

The world around us is a feast of allurement. It is a playground of delights, a sea of joy. Every day we are invited. Will we jump into this sea? Or will we sit as a spectator on the banks? The great Christian writer C. S. Lewis talks of the temptation to ever only dabble at the edges of this vast sea of our joy.

This is my endlessly recurrent temptation: to go down to that Sea . . . and there neither dive nor swim nor float, but only dabble and splash, careful not to get out of my depth and holding on to the lifeline which connects me with my things temporal.[22]

Whether awakening to the morning and lying in bed with the window open to remember our night dreams at the first sleepy trills of birdlife, or taking time to journal our thoughts, or lingering over supper with our children, asking them to recount the day's highs and lows, or taking a long bath with our beloved to share intimate secrets—such simple playful activities can awaken a new sense of joy. In our fast-track culture that deadens our senses for Sabbath play, it takes time to cultivate this particular joy within us. But when we participate in play, joy pops up in our daily interactions, moment by moment, seeding its mysterious ways within our heart. Playtime begins to shrink the exaggerated importance of our steroid-driven lives down to size. As the delighted and playful thirteenth-century Sufi sage Hafiz says, "What is this love and laughter bubbling up from within me?" The reply: "It's the sound of a soul waking up!"[23]

LEISURELY WORK

As a product of my culture, I had no consciousness of "leisurely work." For me, leisure was a two-week vacation. It was the secular idea of working until you feel the burn and then going far away. Preferably to a tropical oasis. It didn't occur to me to take time out from a busy day at work to take a short, mindful walk or to sit and watch a blue jay hide acorns for winter. But one writing day, laughing as I watched silly bluebirds chase chipmunks around a woodpile in a "king of the mountain" game, I began to see Sabbath keeping as spacious moments sprinkled throughout. These could enrich a whole workday with joy. Taking time for such moments often shifted my mood. Work looked different upon return. A Sabbath mind was growing in me. Joy was seeping into my work life, rerouting my neurons.

Brother David Steindl-Rast believes that leisure does not need to be divorced from work. We should be able to have leisurely work. According to him, the opposite of work is not leisure. It is play. And reclaiming play introduces leisure into all aspects of our life, including work. Steindl-Rast says:

> Work is something we do to accomplish a purpose
> that lies outside the activity itself; once the purpose is
> accomplished the activity ceases. . . . Play is something

we do because we find meaning in it, an activity which has all its purpose within itself. . . . Leisure introduces into every activity an element of play . . . doing whatever it be also for its own sake, not only to get it done. Thus leisure provides the climate in which one can be open for meaning.[24]

In the final years of my ministry, I began to practice something called *worshipful work*. With the encouragement of my teachers, I began to incorporate time into each church committee meeting for sharing joys and concerns or a brief devotional to center our attention. Though at first there were questioning glances and uncomfortable silence, soon enough I could see that it changed the tenor of the meetings. There was less tension in me and hopefully my members felt that too. Soon I noticed that our new conference minister was no longer doing business as usual. When we gathered for our annual meeting, we didn't sit for hours churning through reams of minutes and documents. We spent most of our time in worship, hanging out, laughing, crying, telling stories with one another. In the lean years of conflict, which came later, we actually remembered that we liked each other and were less determined to oust the one who saw things differently. The winds of change were making a difference. Meaning was being created anew. Joyful space was being created in worship and work.

The biblical Sabbath brought work and leisure together, side by side, early on. Practicing Sabbath leisure could introduce play and meaning into work and all of life. Good work was not to be diminished, its serious enterprise was not to be erased, only put in perspective. We are all workers—contributing in some way. But we all deserve rest. God's blueprint for leisure was not for only the wealthy landowners and the well-heeled. Actually, the ones it benefitted the most were those in the trenches, the servants, the manual laborers, the oxen, and the land worked daily to turn a profit. Sabbath was instituted first and foremost for the common man and woman. After the oppression of the Hebrews in Egypt, Sabbath was more than just a nice concept for a balanced life with good vacations. It was about freeing people from work that enslaved. Biblical Sabbath leisure was about tending a quality, a way of being beyond simply taking time off. It was about remembering a God who created leisure and then going out and experiencing it.

In secular society through the centuries, meaningful leisure required gobs of disposable time, which limited it to the wealthy. For the masses, work had become increasingly industrialized and meaningless. But the advent of labor unions in the United States and around the developed world meant jobs with benefits and forty-hour workweeks. It reintroduced leisure to the masses. Workers could have access to sick-day benefits, two weeks of paid vacation, and retirement benefits to ensure a happy old age. Sports fans—whether as spectators or participants—could enjoy baseball every weekend, or pickup soccer and Ultimate Frisbee in the park with friends. Hobbyists could enjoy bird watching, antique browsing, and gardening for pleasure. Secular culture successfully reclaimed Sabbath for the worker as well as the wealthy. It reinvigorated the meaning, the *why*, of working. Compensation was more than just money. It was time.

As I hung up my stoles for the last time and boxed up my office from thirteen years of ministry, I would need to reimagine work for myself and find meaning in how I related to a culture that continued on with the same work paradigms that I had left. Meanwhile I joined the unchurched crowd on Sunday morning. No longer did I need to get up like clockwork on Sunday morning and spend the lion's share of my day at church. At first I felt a pang of guilt when family or friends asked where I attended church now that I was a free agent. When I responded that I was taking a break, they would all hide their temporary surprise and quickly move along. I was no longer the "church lady."

Though I missed the rhythm of the church seasons and the collective celebration of keeping Sunday Sabbath, I knew that the container of "going to church" didn't necessarily ensure a joyful life. What made the difference was keeping a day set aside, any day, to grow my Sabbath mind, a place to truly connect with God and my own hungry soul. As joy opened like a flower in me, I would need to find good work again. But my work ethic was being dismantled. I was in territory with new explorations of the meaning of work. Eventually I stopped feeling guilty for no longer being a part of the regular nine-to-five workforce moving out into the world each day. But I knew that I was on shaky ground. All my money fears were showing up. I would need to examine what I believed about the work paradigm I had been plugged into my whole life. I felt the danger and risk of this time. I was also exhilarated by the possibilities.

Tending Your Sabbath Soul

1. How do you cultivate joy in your life? What would it take to jump into the sea of your delight?

2. How does creativity play a role in your life? What would a day, a week, or even a month dedicated to your creativity look like?

3. How might Sabbath keeping open up new avenues of play in both your professional and your personal life?

4. What is your understanding and even manifestation of leisure in your life and work? Is "leisurely work" a foreign concept or one you embrace or experience in your life?

6

REIMAGINING WORK
God's Sabbath Economy

The Sabbath is a day for the sake of life. Man is not
a beast of burden, and the Sabbath is not for the
purpose of enhancing the efficiency of his work.
—ABRAHAM JOSHUA HESCHEL, *The Sabbath*

STOPPING WORK,
TRUSTING IN "ENOUGH"

Sabbath keeping brought me to this point in my life. It helped
me discern that it was time to leave a job that gave me a decent
living and meaningful work but left me wanting for more creative
space in my life. Now I am on a new path of equally wonderful
work, but without the safety net of a regular paycheck—for now.
Observing Sabbath opened up Pandora's box to explore things
unnoticed and unknown about myself. But it also introduced me
to the underground world of alternative economies. Now, down
on the canyon floor after jumping off the professional cliff, I am
facing a whole host of assumptions about the work economy that
I had taken as gospel. One is that the economic model I feed is
the only one available. Another is about "enough."

Since I've left congregational ministry, I have been
schooled in God's Sabbath economy of "enough." I no longer

buy tea lattes and hang out at coffee shops. I just don't have the spare change. Like most, I find that the more I earn, the more I spend. Must be a human thing. So now that I don't have the income I'm accustomed to, I'm beginning to explore an "enough" that isn't calibrated on external income. It's based on an inner and intrinsic discipline of limits. Once, I visited a women's hospital in Ethiopia that received a portion of their funding from a church in the United States. A group of young people had decided to save their collective money from former daily latte runs to buy hospital medical equipment in order to provide free health care to poor rural women. I wish I could say I'm doing this. It is a vision of enough—in service of others. These days I carefully count my pennies and live low on the food chain of consumerism. I have everything I need. I don't need more sweaters or shoes. Or this or that amazing gadget. My husband still laments all the accumulated "stuff" crammed in our closets from years of purchasing power. I hope to get to it someday soon.

A RESISTANCE MOVEMENT

To understand the roots of God's Sabbath economics we must return to the story of the enslaved Israelites, making bricks for Pharaoh's empire and its hungry beast of production.[1] Moses, post–burning bush, led his people into forty years of wilderness exile. There they entered God's Sabbath Economy 101. The newly uprooted Hebrews, unmoored from their life, stuck in a desolate wilderness, were waking up. They were not Pharaoh's fodder. They were YHWH's beloved community.[2] It was not a pretty sight. According to the story, there was lots of teeth gnashing, complaining, and kicking against this new existence. Learning to trust and hear God's dreams for a just society and a new "enough" for their life was, let's just say, painful. It's never easy to let go of the "fleshpots of Egypt," to give up the security of all we've known for the promise of what could be.

Eventually Sabbath keeping made its way into a book of commandments that Moses brought down off Mount Sinai. It was the fourth commandment, and it was an important one for Israelites who for four hundred years had been slaves. More than just a nice idea, Sabbath keeping became a flagship of resistance. It reminded God's people of how God had pulled the plug on their slavery to the ceaseless, insatiable labor machine of the Egyptian empire. That economic model would be rendered impotent in the wilderness. Instead there was God's economy, at the heart of which was a blueprint for Sabbath rest. It honored all laborers, including animals and the soil. The goal was to loosen the bonds of a tyrannical economic system where resources flowed only upward, to those in power. The cycles were in sevens: Every seven days you shall rest, because the Lord rested after seven days of creation. Every seven years you shall observe an extended Sabbath, allowing the land, animals, and humans to rest from labor for a year.

Theologian Barbara Brown Taylor sees Sabbath keeping as more than rest. It is active resistance to the exploitation of others and the exhaustion of the land. "When you stop working, so do your children, your animals, and your employees. . . . By interrupting our economically sanctioned social order every week, Sabbath suspends our subtle and not so subtle ways of dominating one another on a regular basis."[3] She goes on to lament that where there is money to be made, there is no rest for the land or those who live on it. Resistance will have to come from those who live by a different rhythm.

Back to the Israelites, when forty-nine years (7 x 7) rolled around, a fiftieth-year Jubilee was proclaimed.[4] Debts were erased. Slaves were emancipated. The productive land lay fallow and the animals rested. This *Shabbat Shabbaton*—literally a double Sabbath—not only gave all laborers time to rest but also demanded that the community wealth be reset and rebalanced. The economic engine was adjusted for human dignity and well-being.

God's economy was about deconcentrating power and wealth at the top. The people were liberated from the steroid demands of the workplace, their hearts were unbound, their minds were decolonized, and their habits were retrained. All God's family deserved to live with enough. And if the wandering Hebrews in the Exodus wilds thought they could begin to capitalize on the simple providence God provided—a daily ration of manna and quails in the desert—they were quickly disabused. They were instructed not to gather more than they needed to feed the community each day because the extra would become a stinking, rotting mess when stashed away. Sabbath keeping was a sea change, contrasting with the economic narratives of endless exploitation and the disease of greed. It was the beginning of biblical justice, meant to bring relief for those who were weary and burdened by an economic engine that ate people up and spit them out. My thoughts return to my own stuffed closets, certainly containing more than I need. I am called to examine my own habits and why I have way more shoes than I can ever wear every season while some people have none or a tattered pair full of holes.

THE GRACE OF LIMITS

The grace of gifts and limits is something a market-driven economy has no use or language for. When profit is the bottom line, limits are heresy. Yet Bible teacher and writer Ched Myers reminds us of this radical nature of God's Sabbath economy:

> At its root, Sabbath observance is about gift and limits;
> the grace of receiving that which the Creator gives, and

the responsibility not to take too much, nor mistake the gift for a possession.[5]

Those who suffer the greatest consequences of a society flouting the wisdom of limits are the most vulnerable, human and creaturely. Pablo Fajardo is an Ecuadorian who grew up poor, working in the Amazon basin for Chevron. Eventually he became a lawyer committed to securing his people's economic and environmental rights in the Chevron oil fields.

> One of the problems with modern society is that it places more importance on things that have a price than on things that have a value. Breathing clean air, for instance, or having clean water in the rivers, or having legal rights—these are things that don't have a price but have a huge value. Oil does have a price, but its value is much less. And sometimes we make a mistake.[6]

When work destroys people's lives and the gifts of the earth, work's true purpose and life-giving outcome is lost. We overstep our limits. Losing sight of a more holistic vision of living, we alienate ourselves from earth as our home and all humans as our kin. Limits are intrinsic to God's Sabbath economy. Sabbath will only reenergize our work insomuch as we allow ourselves to examine our own excess and put boundaries around our work. How do we find balance between meaningful work and much needed rest for people, animals, and the earth's resources, rather than accepting an unlimited enterprise to privatize and exploit for profit?

Once I had unplugged from the economy of wages, I stood terrified at what I had done. Where would I get my daily bread? I had been given a grant for a writing project, but it lasted only a short time. What would I do after that? I still lived in a monetized society after all.

Funny thing—as work stress fell away in great swaths, and my time became like an open meadow on Sabbath, I began to dream new dreams. Perhaps they were God's dreams. I was given the inner guidance to begin writing grants. And so I did. Fast and furious. I created a small organization called Think Like a Bee (www.thinklikeabee.org). I churned out enough money to fund it. Sabbath mind sustained me. Mysteriously, what I needed began to show up as I recharted my course. I had enough to contribute my part to our household bills each month.

UNLOADING CRUSHING DEBT

God's Sabbath economy is also about facing the reality of debt in our culture. Our federal government has modeled debt in the trillions. Consumer spending is regularly lauded to prop up the economy. Many in our society have bought into the lie of living beyond our means. We work hard at playing this game, deluding ourselves into believing we have a bigger slice of the pie by over-extending ourselves through debt.

Before I entered ministry as a vocation, I was a social worker and then a seminary student. Attending seminary in the San Francisco Bay area was an experiment in creative economics. This part of California has one of the highest costs of living in the United States; I acquired a lot of debt residing there. In my thirties I dabbled in network marketing, experimenting with the idea of residual income, which I am sure bewildered my industrious, blue-collar, working-class family members. To them, good work involved a reasonable compensation for one's time and energy. My father often moonlighted to keep the family afloat. My mother worked at the same job for over twenty years. Manual labor, farming, nursing, teaching, and family-owned retail were the fabric of our small-town society and class. Consumer loyalty was valued. Rather than working with balanced books, I used credit cards to shore up my flagging finances at school and in my network marketing enterprise. I ended up declaring bankruptcy before finally moving away from California. I was ashamed by what felt like wishful thinking and inexperience rather than good fiscal grounding. This season of life bore hard lessons about acquired debt. It felt like a form of insanity. It took away my freedom to live fully and serve the world's needs rather than the bank. I knew the visceral, erosive anxiety of being indebted. I knew how soul crushing it could be.

One of the biggest problems in the ancient Near East was debt. People became indebted as they were dispossessed of their ancestral land by wealthy landowners. In this unjust system, people worked endlessly to pay off something they never could. Like our credit card system today, and the corruption of the housing market, it destroyed people's lives and kept them in bondage to ceaseless labor.

Jubilee was about unloading debt. One of the beautiful things that emerged in my final years with my congregation was an experiment in Jubilee economics. A small group in our congregation met to study the concept of Jubilee and share their stories of debt. They created a collective plan that each person would pay into and "gift" to one group member at a time. This would go around the circle until everyone had the amazing opportunity of having their debt burden eased. This experiment with creative economics piqued my interest. Without debt and with community support, one could begin to restructure life in a way, hopefully, that was life giving and within limits.

Centuries after the Exodus, Jesus would teach, "Do not worry about your life, what you will eat or drink; or about your body, what you will wear. Is not life more than food, and the body more than clothes?" (Matthew 6:25). I was learning that this idea of not stocking up more than was needed and living free from the burden of debt was a core concept of God's Sabbath economy. But without a like-minded community it could backfire. If individualism prevailed, then the trust of caring for one another and sharing would fall by the wayside. Indigenous communities through the centuries knew how to do this. Today the potlatch ceremony is still strong in the communities of the Northwest. The concept of potlatch is to give away gifts from your own household, an action that supports the belief that wealth is not to be possessed but ultimately shared.

As I left my regular paycheck, I began to notice the barter system as integral to God's Sabbath economy. This gift economy is about sharing and bartering our energy and time for goods. Rather than relying on debt to meet our needs, we work with what we have, exchanging goods and services for another's goods and services. Baskets overflowing with fresh eggs and produce are exchanged for a massage. Traditional medicine treatments are exchanged for basic carpentry services. Together, the community supports each other, resisting overextension that leads to debt, and everyone has enough. Little by little I was learning to trust.

TRUE WEALTH

I had assumed it was financial suicide to leave my ministerial post and the work economy to tend what the Sabbath fires had begun to kindle in me. Even more so if I left in the second half of life when retirement loomed close at hand. Perhaps it was financially insane, but I was ready to challenge work models and an economy that had become like dead weights around my neck. I had begun to suspect that the idea that true wealth lay in benefits, income, and retirement packages was false. Instead this so-called true wealth felt like an endless cycle of dis-ease. As author, satirist, and radio personality Garrison Keillor summarizes, "Life is messy and it always has been. We work hard to earn money, we neglect our health and then we pay the money to restore our health, meanwhile we forgot how to enjoy life, so what good is health anyway."[7]

By the end of my tenure with my congregation, as I was heading into the abyss of no income, I understood that true wealth was community. It was my relationships and friendships that sustained my spirit and animated a network of possibilities for my future. I wasn't looking for a job, but for time to create from the inside out, rather than the outside in. I had shed the weightiness of holding up parts of church structure that I no longer believed in and could no longer defend. I had no desire to be the lightning rod for issues or have my time and energy used up by endless meetings and "administrivia." Now I could just spend time with people, always my favorite part of ministry. Relationships take time to nurture. Sabbath is all about time.

The vast social circles and connections that I had prided myself on, thanks to my work and social predisposition, fell away as I left ministry. I longed to focus on deepening a few relationships—including a relationship with my own soul. My relationship with my husband would also benefit from this righting of priorities. Old Testament scholar Walter Brueggemann explains that the map for the original Sabbath economy was established by a God who values relationships:

> This God is subsequently revealed as a God of mercy, steadfast love, and faithfulness who is committed to covenantal relationships of fidelity. . . . At the taproot of this divine commitment to relationship (covenant) rather than commodity (bricks) is the capacity and willingness of this God to rest.[8]

I like to think I have withdrawn these days from a commodity-driven economy and thrown myself more fully into an alternative economy whose primary value is relationship, but that would be false. I have only scratched the surface. Though God's Sabbath economy has begun to tear apart the economic assumptions and standards I had set my life in accordance with, I still struggle to understand how enmeshed I am.

LAYING DOWN CLATTERING COMMERCE

In my new jobless life outside of ministry, I was also facing another myth of the economic model we live within. We believe our job is to give all our life energy to the clattering looms in the factory without a break. We must do this to keep the economy on track. One day, we begin to think that the looms are all that matter and we are merely there to keep them going.

Sabbath asks us to stop our frenzied work and consuming pace because participating in commerce is not what we were ultimately created for in this life. This letting go can involve wrestling with our own egos as well as discomfort with what is familiar. As Abraham Joshua Heschel puts it:

> He who wants to enter the holiness of the day must first lay down the profanity of clattering commerce, of being yoked to toil. He must go away from the screech of dissonant days, from the nervousness and fury of acquisitiveness and the betrayal in embezzling his own life. He must say farewell to manual work and learn to understand that the world has already been created and will survive without the help of man. Six days a week we wrestle with the world, wringing profit from the earth; on the Sabbath we especially care for the seed of eternity planted in the soul. The world has our hands, but our soul belongs to Someone Else.[9]

A friend who is a spiritual director, blogger, poet, and dancer also freelances as an editor. The work is ever present and only twenty steps away in her home office. With the heart of an artist but a significant Protestant work ethic, she struggles like all of us to balance work and rest. In her blog one day, I stumbled across a good example of how she had come to put clattering commerce in its place. She shared research indicating that five hours is the limit for good, focused, and fruitful attention to work. The returns diminish after five hours of intense concentration. The work space erodes into paper pushing, bathroom visiting, Internet gazing, and other modes of distraction. I can relate. I realized that the more time spent now, post-ministry, in dedicated Sabbath unplugging, the more I have a laserlike readiness for the work that awaits me. I no longer need to spend time escaping work through distractions. When I spend time caring for that "seed of eternity planted in the soul," I return to work refreshed and revitalized.

Evelyn Underhill, known for her compendiums on mysticism and spiritual development, writes beautifully of the need to retreat from the violence of busyness and noise in our world. Invoking the image of the industrial age, Underhill says that our civilization gets more noisy and complex by the day:

> We must not bother about anything else . . . man [*sic*] will get ever more utilitarian . . . wholly forget[ting] his true relationship to God. . . . Even religion tends to become more and more pragmatic and utilitarian; more and more active, and less and less inward, more and more a chain of doings, less and less of an attachment to a being. . . . He has become the slave of the clattering loom. He can't hear his own soul speak.[10]

These days I work on my own schedule. Unplugged from the regular world of wages, I am aware how challenging it is to lay down clattering commerce. At any given moment, I can spend endless hours surfing social media, reading books, cleaning my house, running infinite errands, taking a new career training course, or researching something to death. I don't. I am in the process of training myself to withdraw from all that vies for my attention and find the kernel of pure, unadulterated focus. Sabbath days and hours help me rest so that when it is time to work, I can more quickly get to the meat of what is most important. I no longer need an external prompt by a hiring committee, boss, or office administrator to get to work. When I have had my day set apart, I am refreshed, eager to put the bit into my mouth and strain against it for the new, curious adventure of the day.

Sabbath first shows up in Genesis 2:2, *not* as a command but as an exemplary way of honoring the muse. The Spirit that hovered over the deep, *ruach* (literally the "wind" or "breath" of God), became the impulse for a massive outpouring of creativity. Resting was how the Creator kicked back and reflected after this gigantic earth-making project. It was a way to acknowledge and reflect upon what had just been created. Sabbath was the balance to good, hard work. The Creator was the model for both the importance of work and the ceasing of labors.

There is a violence that we do to ourselves when we ignore Sabbath rest. Even if it is for serving the greater good. As Thomas Merton noted:

> The rush and pressure of modern life are a form, perhaps the most common form, of its innate violence. To allow oneself to be carried away by a multitude of conflicting concerns, to surrender to too many demands, to commit oneself to too many projects, to want to help everyone in everything, is to succumb to violence. The frenzy of our activism neutralizes our work for peace. It destroys our own inner capacity for peace. It destroys the fruitfulness of our own work, because it kills the root of inner wisdom which makes work fruitful.[11]

Bestselling author Wayne Muller writes, "A 'successful' life has become a violent enterprise." When we are always living from a survival mode, decisions are made from a place where everything is a "maelstrom [of] speed and accomplishment, consumption and productivity."[12] He cites the training that medical students go through in particular. A frightening thought to consider how exhausted your attending physician might be, who must make life-or-death decisions.

We are not the dominators. The bottom line of God's Sabbath economy ultimately calls us to live out justice and mercy, which includes being merciful and just to ourselves.

ORA ET LABORA

In God's Sabbath economy, prayer and connection to the I AM—not money—is the fountainhead of work. The Benedictines have always understood that prayer and work are two sides of the same coin. *Ora et labora*, Latin for "prayer and work," reveals the critical nature of pairing the two together—weaving right livelihood with one's spiritual nature. Social justice activist, lecturer, and bestselling author Catherine Doherty writes, "Without prayer, the life of the Christian dies."[13] Lauren Winner, commenting on Doherty's words, says, "The problem is that your Christian life gets sick before it dies, and it is hard to keep praying when you are sick."[14] When something in us dies, our work suffers. It becomes meaningless. Prayer is the antidote for the sickness of heart that leaves us stranded from God.

In his book *Christ of the Celts*, spiritual teacher and author John Philip Newell draws from fourteenth-century mystic Julian of Norwich when he talks about this sickness as a love-longing, our "sacred longing for union" with God:

> [This love-longing] is the most sacred and natural of yearnings. The deeper we move within the soul, the

closer we come to this divine yearning. And the nearer we come to our true self, [as Julian of Norwich says,] "the greater our longing will be."[15]

If this love-longing is not healed or nourished, it becomes irritated and inflamed as a wound in our life. It can draw us to things that aren't life giving. Alexander Scott, the nineteenth-century Celtic teacher, used a plant suffering from blight to talk about the human condition. Botanists would never refer to the essence of the plant based upon its blight, but rather would identify the healthy properties of height, color, scent—the blight is only an unfortunate illness or disease that took over as the original beauty and health of the plant was compromised.[16] But not so with us. We have become so accustomed to our blighted human condition that we don't see the beauty of our souls or of one another and the whole creation. In our trancelike amnesia, we have come to accept that this is just the way it is. Rather than being a natural outflowing from the soul's essence, connected with our Divine Source, work loses its true meaning.

This love-longing was like a prayer in me many times when I escaped for extended Sabbath. Saint Augustine (354–430 CE) spoke about prayer as that which comes from our deepest desire for God:

> The desire of your heart is itself your prayer. And if the desire is constant, so is your prayer. The Apostle Paul had a purpose in saying: "Pray without ceasing." Are we then ceaselessly to bend our knees, to lie prostrate, or to lift up our hands? Is this what is meant in saying: "Pray without ceasing"? Even if we admit that we pray in this fashion, I do not believe that we can do so all the time.

Yet there is another, interior kind of prayer without ceasing, namely, the desire of the heart. Whatever else you may be doing, if you but fix your desire on God's Sabbath rest, your prayer will be ceaseless. Therefore, if you wish to pray without ceasing, do not cease to desire.[17]

Similarly, the short breviary published by Saint John's Abbey exhort us:

The flame of love is the heart's cry. Love always and you will always cry out; cry out always and you will always desire; desire always and you will always remember the rest that awaits you.[18]

A mantra that devout Muslims repeat in the midst of their work is *Subhan Allah, Al-hamdulillah, Allahu Akbar* ("Glory be to God, Praise be to God, God is Great"), a constant and unceasing reminder of whom this world belongs to. Several times a day, in the midst of their work worlds, Muslims bow in prayer, an act of deepening intimacy between God and the human being. As the Prophet Muhammad says, "The freshness of my eyes is given to me in prayer."[19]

Prayer was a balm at the Benedictine monastery in northern New Mexico where I began to recover from the violence of my own busyness. It was an antidote for my soul, along with the work and prayer rhythm that the monks practiced. It gave me a new idea for how I could balance my work life with silence—stopping what I was doing to listen to a different voice. In the Sufi tradition, "sages say that silence is the language of God: everything else is a poor translation."[20] Prayerful silence is not an easy practice in the beginning. I was assailed by lists, sometimes by emotions long tamped down and locked up. Silence opened me to my grief and anger in a world of suffering. I quickly wanted to migrate back to my distractions or techno toys to stop the assault—my monkey mind immediately droning on in that gaping place of quietude. It was an annoyance, but with patience and practice of a silent mantra, breathing, and yoga, I began to compassionately observe and release these things. I became more committed than ever to these practices in the wake of leaving ministry. Grounding my days in these ways was the only way to sustain my endeavors. It was one of the great gifts that burnout taught me.

Sometimes it seems that we who could use silence and solitude the most are often the farthest away from it. Prayerful silence and solitude seem beyond our grasp. I think of the overworked employee, the teen plugged into an iPhone, the overwhelmed, multitasking parent. We have not taught the members of our churches, synagogues, or mosques that it is okay to embrace silence for even a few minutes, or an hour, much less take a whole Sabbath day from our crazed, frantic lives. So we carry on in the empty noisiness of our culture. But when we seize time for silence, our desire for God can grow, though it is always an imperfect process.

Richard Rohr, Franciscan priest, author, and teacher, talks about preparing for failure when one sits down in silence to pray. Because of the inner resistance we often encounter when we try to pray, we often give up before we experience its fruits. For us to reap the benefits of prayerful silence, we must begin with baby steps. Experiment. There are so many ways to pray.[21] But you don't need to be fancy. As in any friendship, just begin by stopping, sitting, listening, making time in the midst of your days. It is in the act of showing up that we have the glimmer of a chance to be transformed.

Prayer at its core is about moving toward what Julian of Norwich called *one-ing*—meeting our hunger for communion and union with the Divine. It is about ultimately moving toward a unitive consciousness with the One whose imprint we bear. If sin is separation and dis-unity that takes us far away from God, then prayer can transport us back to that home of our deepest longing. Until God becomes our foundation, we will always fall back on our own self-righteousness and clever schemes. Until it all falls apart . . . As Rohr says:

> What we're doing in prayer is letting our self-made foundation crumble so that God's foundation can be our reality. Prayer is a practice in failure that overcomes our resistance to union with Love. Let's fall into and rest in that Love one more time.[22]

I learned centering prayer, revived by Trappist monk Thomas Keating, during my time in ministry. It is a method of silent meditative prayer with a sacred word as a mantra, preparing us to receive the gift of Divine Presence. Keating sees it as a way for the Divine Therapist to come and heal our life as we empty ourselves of our ego mind and listen for God's whisperings. This method of prayer forges a relationship with God's Spirit and a discipline to foster that relationship. The goal is to sit for at least twenty minutes twice a day with a sacred word or with the breath as a mantra, as a way to open up to God's presence. Today I still find this challenging. The ideal is for our "soul's forgetfulness" to awaken little by little into our true eternal essence.[23] The Spirit is within us, closer than breathing, closer than thinking, closer than consciousness itself. Despite the challenges, I have found over the years that with this practice I can weave prayer throughout the workday.

Spiritual director David Frenette wrote about the core of Christian contemplation:

> If you asked me for just one bit of advice about contemplation, I would say to practice the meaning of the word "amen." . . . In the Western religions [it is used]

to express profound faith, to assent to the Mystery, to surrender to God. . . . Amen means, literally, "so be it" or "let it be." With amen, your words and actions yield to God's presence.[24]

Perhaps a whispered "amen" in the midst of our labors would realign our vocation with God's will, changing our concept of ourselves in the world, on the planet.

The work of prayer is in service of work, and likewise, work is in service of prayer. Without prayer and the structures of spiritual practice, I would be sucked into the mania of our culture, falling away from my own recovery from the type-A workaholism that our culture glorifies. And without good work in the world, I would fall into narcissistic navel gazing. Over time, balancing the practice of Sabbath prayer and silence with work became an oasis for my soul in the changing fortunes and tides of our time. Now, instead of collecting as many glittering things as possible in my life, prayer helps me keep a balanced state of mind and heart in my daily work life. My inner authority has grown up. I find myself less vulnerable to social and economic forces, the addictiveness of a culture demanding my mindless allegiance. Though I continue to be a passionate person whose first impulse is to take on as many righteous causes as I can muster, when I pay attention to my deepening desire for God, the creative life, work, and nourishing relationships flow in right alignment. Work becomes rooted in deeper spiritual values and meaning—based upon the things that matter most.

HOLINESS, OUR TRUE WORK: TO HEAL AND RESTORE THE WORLD

You've heard it said that hindsight is 20/20. Now that I have some distance from the ministry container, I see it as only *one* of many avenues for doing this work of healing and restoring the world. In God's Sabbath economy, a postal worker, a teacher, a nurse, an activist, a tailor, a garbage collector, and a field hand can heal and restore the world if they see their life as a vehicle for prayer. While I was in it, ministry seemed like the most holy of vocations—spirituality was built into its very job description. *The Minister's Handbook*, in my Mennonite tradition, talked about this calling as specially ordained in the scripture. I saw that it could be a big stage for ego to be inflated. Power paired with anything that has to do with religion or spirituality calls for tremendous humility, lest we fall into the trap of moral superiority and judgment. Thankfully, my congregation kept me humble. Some of the most potent persons I've met, who bring healing and restoration to the communities where they live, have no highly touted office or handsomely compensated role. They are workers with lives of small societal scope but large spiritual impact. I wonder, do they take Sabbath regularly? Maybe they have been nurturing a Sabbath mind for a lifetime.

If people of faith began to see their true vocation as a vehicle of love, not a job description, how would it change our economy and coworkers in the workplace? Work would no longer be simply for commerce and turning a buck, but a place where the Spirit of Creation transforms our lives with justice, peace, and compassion.

Holy literally means to make whole, to heal and be healthy. This is a reorienting of work. Good work and right livelihood matters. We will spend most of our life at work. But if our vocation is not intertwined with the Great Worker, we will not bring holiness into our workaday life no matter what we do.

According to peace activist and author Rabbi Amy Eilberg, vocation in the Jewish faith can be seen as an extension of the Hebrew Bible's exhortation to "be holy because I, the Lord your God, am holy" (Leviticus 19:2). All people, not just people of the cloth, are called to the holy work of cleaving to God—to live an enlightened and elevated ordinary life. To move toward holiness in the midst of the workplace requires us to commune with the One who has ordered and exemplified work in the first place. It is not necessarily about discerning the "right" job or the perfect profession that God has chosen for us. Instead it has to do with living attentively and serving Love in all we do—remembering that everything we undertake is holy. In all our labors lives the seed of our vocation—to live in right alignment with God. Vocation and right livelihood then flow from this understanding and experience. Sabbath keeping in the Jewish world is one of the ways to sanctify and make holy the other six days of our workweek. As the poet and activist Alice Walker said, "Anyone can observe the Sabbath, but making it holy surely takes the rest of the week."[25]

As a minister with two master's degrees, I had changed classes from my parents and grandparents, becoming a white-collar worker whose work seemed to never end. Like my teacher husband, I would take work home. Hourly wages and time clocks no longer dictated the boundaries of when work ended. As a salaried employee, time became a precious commodity, more than physical energy exerted. The lines blurred around work boundaries. When I worked and when I stopped were never clear. My working-class ethic, combined with my femaleness, made me overly conscientious—in the beginning, I rarely took any time off. Since I was not doing manual labor, ceasing work for twenty-four hours would not necessarily give me rest. I needed to relearn ways to withdraw from the constant swirling thoughts in my brain and the stress in my body in order to be of any earthly good in my ministry. Physical activity in nature cleared me out. Still does. God lived there 24/7. As Mary Oliver says, "For me the door to the woods is the door to the temple."[26] The Sunday Sabbath of my childhood was a *day* to rest from manual labor. As a white-collar professional, a day of rest became a *way* of creating Sabbath mind. A slightly different spin on how I knew it as a child.

Shabbat Shabbaton, double Sabbath, is about an inner Sabbath stance. It is *fully* inhabiting Sabbath as time with God so that when we return to the workplace, it is infused with this holy scent. Rabbi Lester Bronstein called *Shabbat Shabbaton* "the essential Shabbat, the root Shabbat." It is more than just a feel-good thing. It's all well and good if the Sabbath observer does feel better, has fun, relaxes, and is refreshed. But more than that, "we should not do Sabbath because it is like the flavor of the month, or the new place to travel, or the latest diet or charitable cause."[27] We should do it because without it we'll be dead. Not physically but spiritually dead. Our spirits need to regularly reconnect with holiness and sacredness. Sabbath is a dedicated time and space to do this. More than a rote ceasing of activity, it is also about being in a receptive mode for an infusion of God.

The fruits of a holy life feed our labors and strengthen us to fulfill our true vocation. For Jews, this is described as repairing the world—*tikkun olam*. We engage our true vocation when we get off the mainstream merry-go-round to pick up the pieces of a broken society and begin the work of mending and healing one another and a planet that is in tatters. When we cease business as usual, we come face-to-face with that which is no longer usual—vast and growing imbalances of wealth between the rich and the poor, melting ice caps and environmental catastrophe, skyrocketing cancer statistics, civil and human rights violations, relationships crumbling in our own lives. Our alienation from God and one another. Endless wars.

Repairing the world takes tremendous courage, soul strength, community, and compassion. This work cannot be done in a healthy way without prayer in our efforts.[28] Being a healing vessel for a broken world, accompanying others whose souls are fragmented, can only truly happen when we have begun our inner healing. We live tedious lives at the mercy of our surroundings, losing the big picture, lost in our to-do lists. We forget about that interior castle that the sixteenth-century Spanish Carmelite nun Teresa of Avila wrote of in her book by the same name. The mysteries of our soul are often alien to us until we begin to visit the rooms of their beauty. There we learn grace, humility, compassion, forgiveness, and more.

To sustain our ability to serve others, it is critical that we also nurture and nourish ourselves. This relationship with self is like putting on your own proverbial oxygen mask as the plane crash-lands before you help another. That is what I eventually learned—often the hard way. Only then can you practice the golden rule for others. As the Prophet Muhammad wrote, "No one of you can be a true believer unless he wishes for his brother what he wishes for himself."[29] Thus the first act of service is to bring love and healing to ourselves, gently and mercifully healing our own suffering and dysfunction. Then we will bring less anger, confusion, and pain into the world. We will have more space inside us to face the other's suffering with understanding, compassion, and mercy. We become peace bearers and peacemakers. Sabbath can offer us this sacred space for our own healing, so we can return to the world ready for our true work of repairing the broken places. We experience and cultivate compassion by spending time in the great and loving heart of God.

Micah, a prophet of old in both the Jewish and Christian testaments, called us to "act justly and to love mercy and to walk humbly with your God" (Micah 6:8). This has been a guiding light for those seeking to walk in the way of compassion and justice. Jesus reminded his followers that this Great Commandment included "Love the Lord your God, *and* love your neighbor as yourself." The Qur'anic invocation "in the name of God, boundlessly compassionate and endlessly merciful" is uttered by devout Muslims as a way of reminding themselves of forgiveness as well as being a call to become compassionate like the All Merciful. Compassion is seen in Islam as the "mother of all divine attributes."[30]

Vocation as restoring the world is beautifully illustrated by Adnan, a devout Muslim who emigrated from Bangladesh to study in America. After his education he was eventually able to find a lucrative job with Microsoft in Seattle. Though he was successful, he longed for something more than money or power could bring.

> One day, while visiting Bangladesh on business, he came across a poor and grief-stricken father who was carrying the dead body of his son aimlessly in the streets. Adnan instinctively wanted to help, but he had appointments to keep so, reluctantly, he traveled on. But the encounter weighed on him and pierced his heart. Something opened up in him and he felt a shift, a turning in a different direction.

It was a Sabbath moment.

> In a sudden burst of awakening, he realized that he had been climbing the wrong ladder. Today, he continues to work at Microsoft, but his motivation is to earn money to fund a nonprofit foundation called Jolkona, which he and his wife established to help the poor and marginalized. Along with his work to serve Allah *zahir* (Divinity manifested in others), Adnan performs spiritual practices to maintain connection with Allah *batin* (the Divinity at the core of his being).[31]

My idea of vocation continues to emerge in this season of my life. As I reimagine my work in God's Sabbath economy, some days are brilliant and clear. I love the newfound flexibility and space for creating. Other days I struggle to make sense of this new path, feeling lost without external affirmation, regular compensation, and structure. My spiritual director, an entrepreneur herself, says that it is a privilege to step into our creativity and freedom. Not many people have the courage nor the stomach for the unpredictability and precariousness of this journey. As I learn about my own internal rhythms, hungers, and needs, I find myself deepening into trust for Providence's mysterious ways. My regular prayer is "Use me for a purpose greater than myself." Sabbath is no longer just reserved for one day a week. I find the threads of Sabbath weaving their ways daily into my habits. As I have tended my Sabbath soul for many years now, Sabbath mind has become second nature. I know when I have "snapped out" of this way of being. I feel out of sorts—alienated from the core of my being. That is when it is time return to that palace in time and remember who I am and whose I am.

Tending Your Sabbath Soul

1. What is your soul's relationship to your work in the world?

2. What constitutes "enough" in your life? Have you hit this sweet spot, or are you still seeking? How might Sabbath help in this balance?

3. God's Sabbath economy is about loosening the bonds of acquisition and greed to deepen into sharing, trust, and relationship. Do you have a story of someone who experienced an epiphany moment in their life, calling them away from their job to a vocation more rooted in Sabbath economy than capitalist economy?

4. Consider the quote by Catherine Doherty, "Without prayer, the life of the Christian dies." What is prayer for you? What is the state of your prayer life?

5. *Tikkun olam* is a way of restoring and repairing the damage of a profit-driven world. How might this concept change your workaday life and your idea of your vocation?

ACKNOWLEDGEMENTS

To my first settled congregation, Albuquerque Mennonite Church. Authentic and loving, you taught me to become a pastor and a writer. Without our shared journey, I would've never discovered Sabbath keeping.

The Louisville Institute, the board and staff, particularly Brad Wigger, Keri Liechty, and Don Richter. For the grants, encouragement, and support to write.

The community at Nada Hermitage in Crestone, Colorado, and the Norbertine Community in Albuquerque. Your epic hospitality and friendship in these beautiful and sacred places grounded my writing.

The Collegeville Institute staff, for inviting me to become a scholar in residence, and giving me almost four glorious months of room and board and writing space. Living on this Benedictine campus brought me back to the rhythms of prayer. The conviviality was amazing—thank you, Carla, Viv, Father Willie, Sr. Theresa, Abbot John Klassen, and all my colleagues.

Stephen Picha, then director of programs at Ghost Ranch, for handing the manuscript to Emily Wichland of SkyLight Paths Publishing, who believed in my work enough to take this to her acquisition team. Thank you, Emily, for your excellence, thoroughness, and kind support when I became bogged down!

Gratitude to the staff at Turner. I love the bees, Maddie! To Jon O'Neal, managing editor, and Stephen and Leslie in Marketing, who welcomed all questions and were generous in spirit and time.

For countless friends and family who have been incredibly supportive, cheering me on. I see your faces. I am grateful.

Finally, to my beloved Kenneth, patient and supportive through this long odyssey of writing and publishing my first book. You set me free while you tended the home fires, welcoming me back with open arms and heart. You teach me soul tending. My eternal love and thanks.

NOTES

Chapter 1: Simplicity

1. Christine Valters Paintner, *Lectio Divina—the Sacred Art: Transforming Words and Images into Heart-Centered Prayer* (Woodstock, VT: SkyLight Paths, 2011), 104.

2. Barbara Brown Taylor, "Sabbath Resistance: Sabbath and the Status Quo," *Christian Century* (May 31, 2005): 35.

3. Ibid.

4. Jamal Rahman, *Spiritual Gems of Islam: Insights and Practices from the Qur'an, Hadith, Rumi & Muslim Teaching Stories to Enlighten the Heart and Mind* (Woodstock, VT: SkyLight Paths, 2013), 17.

5. Evelyn Underhill, "Abba: Meditations Based upon the Lord's Prayer," *The Fruits of the Spirit* (New York: Morehouse, 1989), 105.

6. John D. Roth, *Choosing against War: A Christian View* (Intercourse, PA: Good Books, 2002), 35.

7. Lauren Winner, *Mudhouse Sabbath* (Brewster, MA: Paraclete, 2003), 6–7.

8. Bernard of Clairvaux, *Sermons on the Song of Songs*, sermon 18.

9. William Johnston, ed. *The Cloud of Unknowing and the Book of Privy Counseling* (New York: Doubleday, 1973), chapter 4.

10. Abraham Joshua Heschel, *The Sabbath* (New York: Farrar, Straus & Giroux, 1951), 6.

11. Thirteenth-century Persian Sufi poet Jalaluddin Rumi, "The Guest House," in *Rumi: Selected Poems*, trans. Coleman Barks, with John Moynce, A. J. Arberry, Reynold Nicholson (New York: Penguin, 2004), 109.

12. Friedrich Nietzsche, *Beyond Good and Evil* (Webster, NY: Millennium, 2014), 46.

Chapter 2: What Makes Your Heart Sing?

1. "The Love of God," by Frederick Lehman, first published in *Songs That Are Different*, vol. 2 (Pasadena, CA: n.p., 1919). The lyrics of verse three are based on the Jewish liturgical poem *Akdamut*, written in 1050 by Meir Ben Isaac Nehorai, a cantor in Worms, Germany. See http://www.hymntime.com/tch/htm/l/o/v/loveofgo.htm.

2. Christine Valters Paintner, *Lectio Divina—the Sacred Art: Transforming Word and Images into Heart-Centered Prayer* (Woodstock, Vermont: Sky-Light Paths), 19–20.

3. Frederick Buechner, *Wishful Thinking* (New York: Harper & Row, 1973), 95.

4. "Logotherapy," Viktor Frankl Institute of Logotherapy; www.logotherapyinstitute.org/about_logotherapy.html.

5. C. George Boeree, "Viktor Frankl," http://webspace.ship.edu/cgboer /frankl.html.

6. Jamal Rahman, *Spiritual Gems of Islam: Insights and Practices from the Qur'an, Hadith, Rumi & Muslim Teaching Stories to Enlighten the Heart and Mind* (Woodstock, VT: SkyLight Paths, 2013), 36.

7. Frederick Buechner, *Now and Then: A Memoir of Vocation* (New York: HarperSanFrancisco, 1983), 87.

8. Wayne Muller, *Sabbath: Finding Rest, Renewal, and Delight in Our Busy Lives* (New York: Bantam, 2000), 6.

9. William Blake, "Auguries of Innocence," available at www.poetryfoundation.org/poems-and-poets/poems/detail/43650.

10. Frederick Buechner, *Telling Secrets: A Memoir* (New York: HarperCollins, 1991), 45.

11. "The honey stains . . . in the ceramic vessels, found 170 kilometers west of Tbilisi [Russia], are believed to be made by bees that buzzed around in Georgia 5,500 years ago—some two thousand years older than the honey found in Egyptian Pharaoh Tutankhamen's tomb, which had been considered the oldest before." Giorgi Lomsadze, "Report: Georgia Unearths the World's Oldest Honey," March 30, 2012, www.eurasianet.org/node/65204.

12. New Catholic Encyclopedia, s.v. "Exsultet Iam Angelica Turba."

13. *The Roman Missal*, 3rd ed. (Collegeville, MN: Liturgical Press, 2011).

14. Robert Bly, trans., *Times Alone: Selected Poems of Antonio Machado* (Middletown, CT: Wesleyan University Press, 1983), 43.

15. Joey Weisenberg, interview by Aryeh Bernstein, "Music as Spiritual Practice: A Conversation," *Sh'ma: A Journal of Jewish Ideas*, April 1, 2014, http://shma.com/2014/04/music-as-spiritual-practice-a-conversation.

Chapter 3: Creation as Sabbath Companion

1. Wayne Muller, *Sabbath: Finding Rest, Renewal, and Delight in Our Busy Lives* (New York: Bantam, 2000), 68–69. Italics in the original.

2. The Hebrew term *nefesh chayyah* is used interchangeably for "living being" and "living creature" in Genesis 2:7, 19 and 7:4—naming both human and animal creatures with the same term.

3. Tertullian, "Caro salutis est cardo," from *De resurrectione carnis* (*Treatise on the Resurrection*) 8, 2. Cited in Richard Rohr, "Infinite Presence, Infinite Love," Center for Action and Contemplation Daily Meditations, November 7, 2016, https://cac.org/infinite-presence-infinite-love-2016-11-07.

4. Richard Rohr, "Infinite Presence, Infinite Love."

5. Mary Oliver, talk at Wellesley College Chapel, October 20, 2010, available at http://naturalwisdom.blogspot.com/2010/10/mary-oliver-at-wellesley-what-beauty-is.html.

6. Pierre Teilhard de Chardin, *The Divine Milieu* (New York: Harper & Row, 1960), 13.

7. Edward Abbey, *Desert Solitaire* (New York: Ballantine, 1968), 169.

8. Richard Rohr, "Nature as a Mirror of God," Center for Action and Contemplation Daily Meditations, November 8, 2016, https://cac.org/nature-mirror-god-2016-11-08. *Scivias* is short for *scito vias Domini*, "know the ways of the Lord."

9. Pierre Teilhard de Chardin, *The Divine Milieu* (New York: Harper & Row, 1960), 41.

10. Albert Schweitzer, *Out of My Life and Thought* (New York: Mentor Books, 1958), 126.

11. Baba Dioum, paper presented at the General Assembly of the International Union for the Conservation of Nature and Natural Resources, New Delhi, 1968.

12. Lauren Winner, *Mudhouse Sabbath* (Brewster, MA: Paraclete, 2003), 46.

Chapter 4: Sabbath Hospitality

1. Beverly Lanzetta, "Spiritual Paths: Via Positiva and Via Negativa," July 29, 2015, http://beverlylanzetta.net/2015/07/29/spiritual-paths-via-positiva-via-negativa.

2. Henri Nouwen, *Reaching Out: The Three Movements of Spiritual Life* (New York: Image, 1986), 71.

3. Caroline Elkins, "Deliverance," review of *Even Silence Has an End* by Ingrid Betancourt, *New York Times*, September 30, 2010, www.nytimes.com/2010/10/03/books/review/Elkins-t.html.

4. Nanette Sawyer, *Hospitality—the Sacred Art: Discovering the Hidden Spiritual Power of Invitation and Welcome* (Woodstock, VT: SkyLight Paths, 2008), 29.

5. Joan Chittister, *Wisdom Distilled from the Daily: Living the Rule of St. Benedict* (San Francisco: HarperCollins, 1990), 40, as quoted in Tom Roberts, *Joan Chittister: Her Journey from Certainty to Faith* (Maryknoll, NY: Orbis, 2015), 54.

6. Jean Vanier, interview by Krista Tippett, "The Wisdom of Tenderness," *On Being*, May 28, 2015, https://onbeing.org/programs/jean-vanier-the-wisdom-of-tenderness.

7. Henri Nouwen, *Intimacy* (San Francisco: HarperOne, 2009), 29.

8. Tim Kreider, "The 'Busy' Trap," *New York Times*, July 1, 2012, https://opinionator.blogs.nytimes.com/2012/06/30/the-busy-trap.

9. Ibid.

10. Jean Vanier, *Community and Growth* (New York: Paulist, 1979), 265.

11. Kreider, "The 'Busy' Trap."

12. Daniel Homan and Lonni Pratt, *Radical Hospitality: Benedict's Way of Love* (Brewster, MA: Paraclete, 2002), 50.

13. Barbara A. Holmes, "Joy Unspeakable in an Unspeakably Joyless World," 2006 Princeton Lectures on Youth, Church, and Culture, available at https://theologytoday.ptsem.edu/uploadedFiles/School_of_Christian_Vocation_and_Mission/Institute_for_Youth_Ministry/Princeton_Lectures/Holmes-Joy.pdf.

14. Barbara Brown Taylor, *An Altar in the World* (New York: HarperCollins, 2009), 40.

15. Ibid., 41.

16. Luke 14:10–17.

17. Jamal Rahman, *Spiritual Gems of Islam: Insights and Practices from the Qur'an, Hadith, Rumi & Muslim Teaching Stories to Enlighten the Heart and Mind* (Woodstock, VT: SkyLight Paths, 2013), 11.

18. C. S. Lewis, *The Screwtape Letters*, letter 9, as quoted in David Fagerberg, "Between Heaven and Earth: C. S. Lewis on Asceticism and Holiness," *Touchstone Magazine* (April 2004): 33.

19. C. S. Lewis, "The Weight of Glory" (sermon), as quoted in Fagerberg, "Between Heaven and Earth."

Chapter 5: Cultivating Joy

1. Sue Monk Kidd, *Firstlight: The Early Inspirational Writings* (New York: Penguin, 2007), 43.

2. Joseph Campbell, *The Hero with a Thousand Faces* (Novato, CA: New World Library, 2008).

3. Jane Vennard, *Fully Awake and Truly Alive: Spiritual Practices to Nurture Your Soul* (Woodstock, VT: SkyLight Paths, 2013).

4. Ibid, 23.

5. Ibid.

6. Mary Oliver, *Upstream* (New York: Penguin, 2016).

7. Ibid., 95.

8. Mary Oliver, *Blue Pastures* (New York: Houghton Mifflin Harcourt, 1995), 2.

9. Ester Buchholz, *The Call of Solitude: Alonetime in a World of Attachment* (New York: Simon & Schuster, 1999), 239.

10. Paula Huston, *By Way of Grace: Moving from Faithfulness to Holiness* (Chicago: Loyola, 2007), xiii.

11. Bob Abernethy and William Bole, eds., *The Life of Meaning: Reflections on Faith, Doubt, and Repairing the World* (New York: Seven Stories, 2007), 143.

12. Anthony de Mello, *One Minute Wisdom* (New York: Doubleday, 1985), 13.

13. Thomas Merton, *New Seeds of Contemplation* (New York: New Directions, 2007), 1. Italics in the original.

14. Ellen Meloy, *Eating Stone: Imagination and the Loss of the Wild* (New York: Pantheon, 2015), 157–58.

15. William Wordsworth, "Ode on Intimations of Immortality," *Recollections of Early Childhood* (1804).

16. Interplay is about unlocking the wisdom of the body, "a global social movement dedicated to ease, connection, human sustainability and play," http://interplay.org.

17. Stuart Brown, interview on *All Things Considered*, "Play Doesn't End With Childhood: Why Adults Need Recess Too," August 6, 2014, www.npr.org/sections/ed/2014/08/06/336360521/play -doesnt-end-with-childhood-why-adults-need-recess-too.

18. Mary Oliver, *Upstream* (New York: Penguin, 2016), 7.

19. Stuart Brown, "Play Doesn't End with Childhood."

20. Diane Ackerman, *Deep Play* (New York: Vintage Books, 1999), 119.

21. Daniel O'Leary, "Threshold of the Soul," *The Tablet* (April 24, 2010): 7.

22. C. S. Lewis, *Screwtape Proposes a Toast and Other Pieces* (New York: Collins Books, 1965), 122.

23. Jamal Rahman, *Spiritual Gems of Islam: Insights and Practices from the Qur'an, Hadith, Rumi & Muslim Teaching Stories to Enlighten the Heart and Mind* (Woodstock, VT: SkyLight Paths, 2013), 193.

24. David Steindl-Rast, *A Listening Heart* (New York: Crossroad, 1983), 25–26.

Chapter 6: Reimagining Work

1. Exodus 1:8–14, 5:6–21 chronicles the oppression of the Hebrews by the Egyptian Pharaoh.

2. A series of consonants in the Hebrew language, YHWH is a vocalization for the unspeakable name of I AM, found in Exodus 16.

3. Barbara Brown Taylor, "Sabbath Resistance: Sabbath and the Status Quo," *Christian Century* (May 31, 2005): 35.

4. In Leviticus 25 and again in Deuteronomy 15, we find the concept of Sabbath and Jubilee. It was a unique system of land ownership and economics within the ancient Hebrew community, designed to redistribute the land and the wealth for the common good, rather than the benefit of the privileged few. During this yearlong Sabbath, the people reverted

to a hunter-gatherer society. There is skepticism about whether this was practiced fully, as eventually the Israelites became an empire themselves, longing for their own king, consolidating power and acquisition of land and human resources.

5. Ched Myers, "Why Sabbath Economics?" *Dove Tales*, vol. 3, no.1 (2005): 1.

6. William Langewiesche, "Jungle Law," *Vanity Fair* (May 2007): 297.

7. Garrison Keillor, "Trump Has Me Searching for a New Religion," *Washington Post*, January 17, 2017, https://www.washingtonpost.com /opinions/?utm_term=.056536ce5660

8. Walter Brueggemann, *Sabbath as Resistance: Saying No to the Culture of Now* (Louisville, KY: Westminster John Knox, 2014), 6.

9. Abraham Joshua Heschel, *The Sabbath* (New York: Farrar, Straus & Giroux, 1951), 13.

10. Evelyn Underhill, "Abba Meditations based on the Lord's Prayer" *The Fruits of the Spirit* (New York: Morehouse, 1989), 105.

11. Thomas Merton, *Conjectures of a Guilty Bystander* (New York: Doubleday, 1965), 81.

12. Wayne Muller, *Sabbath: Finding Rest, Renewal, and Delight in Our Busy Lives* (New York: Bantam, 2000), 4.

13. Catherine Doherty, *Poustinia: Encountering God in Silence, Solitude and Prayer* (Combermere, ON: Madonna House, 2000), 10.

14. Lauren Winner, *Still: Notes on a Mid-Faith Crisis* (New York: HarperOne, 2012), 67.

15. J. Philip Newell, *Christ of the Celts* (San Francisco: Jossey-Bass, 2008), 69.

16. Ibid., 11–12.

17. St. Augustine's sermon on Psalm 37:13–14 in *Days of the Lord: The Liturgical Year*, vol. 1, trans. Gregory LaNave and Donald Molloy (Collegeville, MN: Liturgical Press, 1991), 128.

18. *Book of Prayer: A Short Breviary* (Collegeville, MN: Saint John's Abbey Press, 1975), 57.

19. Jamal Rahman, *Spiritual Gems of Islam: Insights and Practices from the Qur'an, Hadith, Rumi & Muslim Teaching Stories to Enlighten the Heart and Mind* (Woodstock, VT: SkyLight Paths, 2013), 9.

20. Ibid., 22.

21. An especially helpful resource here is Richard Foster's *Prayer: Finding the Heart's True Home* (New York: HarperCollins, 1992).

22. Richard Rohr, "Failing and Falling in Love," Center for Action and Contemplation Daily Meditations, October 22, 2016, https://cac.org /path-descent-weekly-summary-2016-10-22.

23. John Scotus Eriugena, one of the great ninth-century Irish teachers of the Celtic world, said we suffer from a "soul's forgetfulness" and Christ comes to reawaken our true nature. See John Philip Newell, *Christ of the Celts*, 9.

24. David Frenette, *The Path of Centering Prayer: Deepening Your Experience of God* (Louisville, CO: Sounds True, 2012), 3.

25. Alice Walker, *In Search of Our Mother's Gardens* (Orlando: Harcourt, 2004), 351.

26. Mary Oliver, *Upstream* (New York: Penguin, 2016), 154.

27. Rabbi Lester Bronstein, "The Inner Shabbat: Shabbat Shabbaton (Everywhere and All the Time)," Yom Kippur 2010, https://betamshalom.org /sites/default/files/site_pdfs/Yom_Kippur_d%27rash_5771-2010-1.pdf.

28. Joel James Shuman and L. Roger Owens, eds., *Wendell Berry and Religion: Heaven's Earthly Life* (Lexington, KY: University of Kentucky Press, 2009), 5.

29. Jamal Rahman, *Spiritual Gems of Islam*, 37.

30. Ibid., 52.

31. Ibid., 20.

SUGGESTIONS FOR FURTHER READING

Brueggemann, Walter. *Sabbath as Resistance: Saying No to the Culture of Now.* Louisville, KY: Westminster John Knox, 2014.

Buchholz, Ester. *The Call of Solitude: Alonetime in a World of Attachment.* New York: Simon & Schuster, 1999.

Foster, Richard. *Prayer: Finding the Heart's True Home.* New York: Harper-Collins, 1992.

Heschel, Abraham Joshua. *The Sabbath.* New York: Farrar, Straus & Giroux, 1951.

Muller, Wayne. *Sabbath: Finding Rest, Renewal, and Delight in Our Busy Lives.* New York: Bantam, 2000.

Myers, Ched. *The Biblical Vision of Sabbath Economics.* Washington, DC: Tell The Word, 2001.

Rahman, Jamal. *Spiritual Gems of Islam: Insights and Practices from the Qur'an, Hadith, Rumi & Muslim Teaching Stories to Enlighten the Heart and Mind.* Woodstock, VT: SkyLight Paths, 2013.

Taylor, Barbara Brown. "Sabbath Resistance: Sabbath and the Status Quo." *Christian Century,* May 31, 2005.

Valters Paintner, Christine. *Lectio Divina—the Sacred Art: Transforming Words and Images into Heart-Centered Prayer.* Woodstock, VT: SkyLight Paths, 2011.

Winner, Lauren. *Mudhouse Sabbath: An Invitation to a Life of Spiritual Discipline.* Brewster, MA: Paraclete, 2003.